Defying Standardization

Defying Standardization

Creating Curriculum for an Uncertain Future

Christopher H. Tienken

ROWMAN & LITTLEFIELD
Lanham • Boulder • New York • London

Published by Rowman & Littlefield
A wholly owned subsidiary of The Rowman & Littlefield Publishing Group, Inc.
4501 Forbes Boulevard, Suite 200, Lanham, Maryland 20706
www.rowman.com

Unit A, Whitacre Mews, 26-34 Stannary Street, London SE11 4AB

British Library Cataloguing in Publication Information Available

Library of Congress Cataloging-in-Publication Data Available
ISBN: 978-1-4758-1563-4 (cloth : alk. paper)
ISBN: 978-1-4758-1564-1 (pbk. : alk. paper)
ISBN: 978-1-4758-1565-8 (electronic)

∞™ The paper used in this publication meets the minimum requirements of American National Standard for Information Sciences—Permanence of Paper for Printed Library Materials, ANSI/NISO Z39.48-1992.

Printed in the United States of America

To Francesca and Gabriella for defying standardization. Don't follow the pack; it is usually wrong. Love always to Allison. Sempre.

Contents

Foreword
Defy Standardization

It is time to defy standardization. The public education community is at a point in the education reform misadventure where it is simply time to step back and become evidence-informed and practical with curriculum design, development, and implementation. Many educators have had enough of the hyper-standardization that is repressing and deskilling them and extinguishing the creativity, innovation, and passion from their students. The results are in, and standardization has been demonstrated to be a flawed paradigm for public education.

We, the dissenting voices of university faculty, schoolteachers, education leaders, parents, community members, and students across the nation, are quite possibly finally being heard. "Optout" has grown from what was first seen as an extreme idea into a mainstream movement. Bureaucrats from state departments of education across the country have been feeling the public pressure over standardized programs like Common Core and have started renaming, revising, or rejecting them altogether in an attempt to escape the pressure. So maybe, just maybe, the collective pushback against the extreme standardization of curricula expectations and student output, by fierce advocates for quality public schooling, might be making a difference.

Those concerned with the health of public education around the globe have been making their voices heard: standardized curricula expectations and high-stakes testing are deeply problematic. Petitions by professional organizations, research reports in the professional literature, stories in the mainstream press, and public demonstrations continue to call for an end to the homogenization of human beings via forced standardization of public education.

The voices of discontent are clear. They say in unison: "No coreless core." We don't want a dehumanizing and oppressive core of standardization that leaves out the humanities, the arts, democratic spirit, creative and strategic thinking, and most other skills and dispositions presented in this book that transcend centuries.[1] Many educators can see and feel the loss of the humanizing and democratizing qualities of public school and many believe that civil rights have been violated in the process, especially those of high-poverty children and youth and those who educate them in socioeconomically depressed areas of the United States.

So, now what? We have before us a new thoughtful, practical book meant to invite conversation, interaction, and ongoing transformation in the lives of educators and students. *Defying Standardization: Creating Curriculum for an Uncertain Future* is an intriguing, useful companion text to any curriculum or education policy course. It's intended to expedite learning with one's constituents, such as students in education leadership and policy preparation and doctoral programs as well as those in preservice teacher preparation programs or any parties interested in the future of public education.

The movement away from standardization and toward customizing, personalizing, and contextualizing the curricular program for your school and district is the intellectual and professional heart and soul of this text. Christopher H. Tienken's rich education experiences and diverse expertise across schools, districts, and universities, and continents, uniquely position him to write this book and offer it as a next step, a step all interested parties can take to defy standardization and create curriculum that will serve the best interests of students now and in the future.

Putting theory into practice, Tienken gives educators, students, and anyone interested in a vibrant public school curricula a framework for understanding the critical edge—the misinformation of standardized education policies and practices that promulgate myths and lies. Single-handedly, this award-winning educator takes the discourse of critique concerning the single most important curriculum issue in recent times—the standardization of education—and guides it to solutions based on evidence and informed professional judgment. Connecting the theory to application, his practical ideas, anchored in the works of progressive giants such as John Dewey, Harold Rugg, and Hilda Taba land the discussion right where it needs to be—within the purview of local control—that embattled district, school, or classroom that we want to believe has a liberating and thus promising road ahead.

Every traveler needs a backpack and compass for pursuing a new direction. So, like me, you probably won't want to just passively consume this handy, reader-friendly toolkit of ideas and applications, you will want to take action based on it. It will challenge beliefs of some readers and ignite reflection for

1. For an extended discussion of the relevant issues, see Tienken, C.H. & Mullen, C.A. (Eds.). (2016). *Education policy perils: Tackling the tough issues*. New York: Routledge & Indianapolis, IN: Kappa Delta Pi Publications.

others. This is not a volume designed to sit on your bookshelf. Tienken wrote this book to help move curriculum design, development, and implementation forward. It does not include recipes or fill-in-the-blank ideas. This volume is for leaders, those curricular entrepreneurs committed to pushing back against standardization in ways that will positively impact students' lives and their future prospects. The catalyst is not only Tienken's creative imagination but also the reader's. In fact, he challenges the reader as a partner to implement the multifaceted intellectual work that he himself practices and has tested in various contexts to make it practice-ready.

Before us is a vision: Advocacy for twenty-first-century leaders in the unlearning, relearning, and new learning of what it means to have the capacity for strength and success in the innovation economy that honors our humanity. In your hands, you now have a compass: *Defying Standardization.*

Carol A. Mullen, PhD
Professor of Educational Leadership
Virginia Tech

Preface

Education bureaucrats across the country peddle the anti-intellectual practice of standardizing curriculum expectations and claim it is the latest education wonder drug to address all student achievement ailments. Miraculously one curricular program and a battery of tests will supposedly level the achievement playing field for all students, regardless of differences in family human capital and community social capital. Standardized curricular outputs are sold to the American public as the only path to guaranteed academic achievement and global competitiveness.

I wrote this book primarily for educators, students, and community members who search for ways to push back against the repressive standardization of thinking taking place within public education and the United States in general. This book is for those who yearn for a vibrant, innovative, and creative school system in which all students are provided opportunities to pursue their passions and interests in ways that will prepare them to be well-rounded individuals and democratic citizens in a global community.

I am increasingly asked questions by parents, community members, and education administrators about the problems with standardization and what can be done. I am particularly concerned by the misunderstanding of the issue on the part of some education leaders about the dangers of standardization and the lack of ideas on how to deal with those dangers. An increasing percentage of school leaders have been professionally raised in the cave of standardization and unquestioningly follow the pre-enlightenment thinking of some state education bureaucrats.

I organized this book to explain the flaws of standardization and provide concrete, research-based, historically anchored ideas and examples of what people can do to provide an innovative alternative to the regressive practices of standardization. The first four chapters of the book dismantle the claims of the imminent demise of American global competitiveness and the importance of international testing rankings. The first part of the book pierces the veil of flawed theories and philosophies that undergird standardization policies and programs.

The second part of the book, chapters 5–7, provides the empirical and historical foundations that support less standardized curriculum and instruction. The chapters present an evidence-informed curriculum paradigm that educators, students, community members, and policy makers can use to guide decision-making and program development. Chapter 5 provides the philosophical, empirical, and theoretical support for creating curricula that develops skills and dispositions needed in an uncertain future. Chapter 6 presents practical, evidence-informed examples for educators, students, and community members to move from theory to action and develop unstandardized curricula even when trapped in a standardized environment. The final chapter provides a structure for the large-scale and long-term development of curricula at the school and district level based on the best available evidence, theories, philosophies, and informed professional practice to defy standardization and create curriculum for an uncertain future.

Acknowledgments

The world looks very different when viewed through the eyes of children. It is a world where everyone is equal, anything is possible, and love is the most important currency. My daughters Francesca and Gabriella allow me a window into that world and I will be forever in their debt for keeping me focused on the things that matter most. They are my ripples of hope. Grazie carusi. My world would be very different if it weren't for the love of my wife, Allison. Once again, all things are possible with love.

I acknowledge gratefully the support from my Rowman & Littlefield editors, Dr. Thomas Koerner and Carlie Wall. Their feedback and encouragement were always on target and delivered in ways that motivated the completion of this work. I appreciate their willingness to engage in this topic. It is easier to follow the standardized crowd, but I am grateful they are not lemmings.

I have been fortunate in my academic career to be guided by two preeminent scholars. Dr. Charles Achilles dedicated his career to improving education for all children. The profession lost a great resource on February 8, 2013, but his spirit lives on in the hundreds of doctoral students and thousands of educators he influenced during his career. I miss you Doc. Likewise, the thirteen years of mentoring by Dr. Daniel Tanner has been a gift that words cannot do justice. The curricular clarity brought about by his work and frequent personal communication keep my thoughts progressively centered and provide ongoing inspiration. His standards are high but he defies standardization.

I would like to thank the Seton Hall University administration, my colleagues in the Department of Education Leadership, Management, and Policy, and my dean, Dr. Grace May, for the ongoing support. Thanks to my graduate assistant (GA) Kevin Majewski for his careful and conscientious reviews of this book. His feedback was invaluable. Every professor should be lucky enough to have a GA like Kevin. I would also like to thank Dr. Danielle Sammarone for her expert review and thoughtful feedback. She helped me clarify ideas and messages within the book.

This book calls for educators, students, and interested community members to defy standardization and create curriculum necessary for democratic life in an uncertain future. I would like to thank the parents, students, teachers, guardians, and other community members who are unwilling to bow at the altar of standardization and have the courage to take action. Many thanks. Keep up the important work. Thanks to #Edtherapy, #Satchat, #Weleaded, #Leadupchat, and other members of my PLN that critique my ideas.

Thank you to my colleagues at the Università di Catania, Sicily, for their ideas and support: Francesco Coniglione, Cristiano Corsini, Marinella Tomarchio, Department Chair Santo Di Nuovo, and Concetta Pirrone. Sandra Chistolini at the Università degli Studi Roma Tre provided many ideas and research on the unstandardized curriculum of Giuseppina Pizzigoni. Chistolini's work on the importance of citizenship and a more humanistic approach to education inspired my thinking.

Thanks to my parents and sister who remain supportive of my work. Thanks to Pappy for explaining how to hang a Woolwich tuxedo. God bless Lucille.

There exist those special places that inspire ideas and defy standardization: Sicily, San Giovanni Montebello "fra il mare e la montagna," Giarre, the balcony at Colinas Turquesa in Playas del Coco, sunsets at Flamingo Beach, Via Lazio, Tao Fitness, Mt. Etna, Murgo Winery, and Sanctuary III @ il Terrazzo-54/B.

Part I

THE FLAWS OF STANDARDIZATION

Chapter 1

One for All

A universal set of curriculum and assessment expectations for all students: Is it the saving grace for public education or just another empty promise from bureaucrats and education charlatans based on junk science and ideology? Who could argue against a guarantee of better academic performance for all public school children via privately developed common curriculum standards and a corresponding battery of commercially prepared tests to measure fidelity of implementation? A standardized education program for improved academic achievement of all students is appealingly logical and it is straightforward to install.

A policy-making body, like a state education agency, develops, copies, and/or purchases a set of curriculum standards that specify expected outputs and then it adopts a one-size-fits-all testing program to monitor implementation and determine the attainment of the standards based on predetermined expectations and student output. Finally, the policy-making body mandates through legislation and administrative code that public school personnel teach the specified standards and administer the tests to monitor student achievement of the standards and judge teacher effectiveness.

The approach is known as performance-guarantee policy making. The policies and practices focus on guaranteed outputs. The outputs are stipulated in the form of curriculum expectations or standards. The current education reform environment is populated with performance-guarantee policies and practices that use standardized curriculum expectations and commercially prepared tests to deliver and monitor the expected output. One set of expectations for all students is the policy response de jure for all that is said to ail public education.

Some intended results of a standardized approach to education policy making include the closure of the so-called student achievement gaps, improving teacher effectiveness, and ensuring all children are college and career ready. The seemingly efficient and linear approach to education policy making is based on the flawed theories of behaviorism and performativity buttressed by the Essentialist philosophy of education (Bredo, 2002; Bryk and Hermanson, 1993; Lyotard, 1985). The policies born from primitive theories of learning and human behavior, beget primitive solutions, like standardized curriculum expectations.

Mechanistic Miracles

The promise of a mechanistic, efficient solution to the perceived pernicious problem of student underachievement and teacher quality has been the irresistible allure of standardized education reform policies for over 100 years (Dewey, 1902). Early programs like the Lancasterian system, monitorial instruction, and the Gary Plan sought to improve the overall output of the system and create cost efficiencies in public education by homogenizing performance outcomes and instructional delivery through a mechanistic assembly-line approach (Callahan, 1962; Rayman, 1981).

As anyone who has been around children for a sustained period of time can explain, there are a myriad of factors that play havoc with a mechanistic and standardized approach to public education. Policies that seek to standardize public education output rarely take into account the variety of inputs involved. Human development, the environment in which children live and develop, the social and human capital they experience and have access to, and countless other nonschool factors make it unwise to treat all students as if they have the same learning needs, passions, interests, access to quality resources, and the supports necessary to fully capitalize on all their education opportunities.

Most examples of contexts in which the standardization of outputs work best are not found in areas focused on human development, but rather in the manufacturing sector. It should come as no surprise that the quality of manufacturing output relies heavily on the quality of the inputs or raw material. Large deviations or variance in the input can result in large deviations in product output in the manufacturing sector (Rao and Bargerstock, 2011). Therefore, most manufacturers carefully control their inputs to maximize their output. They reject inputs that will not result in maximum output.

The Problem

Although performance-guarantee policies that mandate standardized curriculum expectations sound logical, the approach has a long history of failure. Standardized curriculum expectations for all students in grades K–12 result in a narrowing of the curriculum in terms of the depth and breadth of subject matter experienced by the students and how they experience subject matter. The formats and levels of difficulty of the content presented in a standardized education environment are themselves standardized, and not easily customized to the students because the customization can lead to deviation from the preset expectations.

Standardized curriculum expectations beget standardized teaching methodology because the format and level of difficulty of the content is highly prescribed, and thus, teacher instruction regresses to the expected output leaving little room for diverse instructional methodologies. Over the long term, standardization of curriculum expectations leads to subject-centered instruction and it results in a system that seeks to force children to conform instead of a system built on the premises of developing creativity and meeting the learning needs of the child.

Standardized curriculum expectations stunt creativity, innovation, complex thinking, and other skills and dispositions necessary for an uncertain future. Standardization of education expectations in general leads to fewer students accessing higher levels of education and has a dampening effect on student cognitive risk-taking. The negative influences of standardized education policies and practices have been known for a long time, yet they persist as if it is the only arrow in the education reform quiver.

Current Conception of Curriculum

Definitions of curriculum abound. The definition that guides the discussion in this book emanates from Tanner and Tanner (2007, p. 99), which in turn emanated from Dewey (1916). Tanner and Tanner (2007) defined curriculum as "that reconstruction of knowledge and experience that enables the learner to grow in exercising intelligent control of subsequent knowledge and experience." Active construction of meaning on the part of the learner is implied in the definition, as is active learning through diverse experiences. The curricular content and the student connect via reciprocal learning relationships. Students learn from curricular experiences, and the curriculum should evolve and be customized based on experiences, passions, and interests students bring to the curriculum.

A common theme that one finds in many of the definitions for curriculum is that curriculum is generally a planned course of study implemented over time. Who does the planning and when, along with the pace of the studies differs depending on the philosophical underpinning of the definition. The conception of curriculum used by proponents of standardization of education outputs and instructional processes is a combination of the cumulative tradition of organized knowledge and measured instructional outcomes. It results in the continuous stacking of knowledge into isolated silos enforced with punitive standardized testing (Tanner and Tanner, 2007, p. 120).

The standardized conception of curriculum is operationalized through one-way transmission of knowledge from the adult to the child with a narrow focus on subject-matter mastery and mental discipline. Mastery is commonly expected to be demonstrated one way, the same way for all students. Standardized mastery and mental discipline combine with efficiency of delivery and resources, prescribed outcomes, and assessment systems focused on behavioral control to form a standardized system of education (Thorndike, 1924). Tanner and Tanner (2007) termed the standardized conception of education as the "doctrine of specificity" (p. 118).

The ultimate ends or objectives of the system are broken into specific measurable outputs at each grade level, marking period, or two-week intervals, to be achieved through standardized methods and monitored with standardized instruments. Each piece of output (e.g., demonstration of student learning) is specified in detail relative to its format and level of difficulty. There is little room for creative expression or innovation of thinking or demonstrating what one has learned. The standardized conception of curriculum is in direct opposition to the conception of curriculum put forth by education philosopher John Dewey.

To paraphrase, Dewey (1916) proposed that curriculum is something that needs to be transformed into usable, transferable knowledge by the teacher and students through a process of reorganization, reconstruction, and reflection (pp. 88–91). Dewey remarked that teachers and students played an active role in the development and transformation of the knowledge. The curriculum is something that must be customized at the local level (Dewey, 1929) by those who develop and experience it. Those people directly involved in the education process should be directly involved in the customization and that starts with local educators and students (Tramaglini and Tienken, 2016).

Dewey's conception of curriculum belies the underlying notions of standardization that curriculum is something that can be developed distally, far removed from the student, and delivered efficiently to the student, who then must dutifully act as a receptacle in which subject matter is deposited. Freier (2000) termed this mechanical conception of education the Banking Model in which isolated and disconnected knowledge is deposited into students' heads, like a transaction. Students must accept the deposit without question.

Regardless of what one calls it, the standardized conception of curriculum violates the nature of the learner as an active constructor of meaning who brings prior knowledge and experience to the learning situation. It violates the precept that students must be able to actively make meaning by connecting their prior experiences and knowledge to the new knowledge and learning experiences (Dewey, 1929). However, students' prior knowledge, experiences, interests, passions, or aspirations are not part of the equation in a system based on a standardized performance expectations, or output-guarantee ideology.

Performance guarantee, or output guarantee as it is sometimes referred to, disregards inputs and attempts to bring about efficiency by specifying, in minute detail, the expected outputs and processes. Much of the complexity and uncertainty of inputs and processes are ignored by standardized performance-guarantee curriculum policies and programs. Proponents of standardization must only set the desired outcome and create a monitoring network for that outcome and the system supposedly runs itself.

"It is like magic; poof! And academic improvement happens." Proponents of standardization claim that equity and equality are ensured because there is one set of performance expectations for all students and education personnel. The same set of expectations for all is the clarion call of standardization, as if all students start and should end in the same place. Standardization of curricular expectations conceals the underlying causes of differences in outputs: differences among the inputs, the students. By ignoring the inputs, standardized programs are inherently systems-centered, not student-centered, yet they appear highly practical and equitable.

Alluringly Simple

Why wasn't the beguilingly practical approach to the very complex problem of education reform legislated prior to 1994? Why did America's children have to wait almost 150 years after the reforms set in motion by Horace Mann (1848) to receive the standardized elixir for superior cognitive, social, emotional, and economic growth? The steady march toward the modern iteration of mass standardization of education outputs through the use of universal curriculum standards and standardized testing predates the majority of the teachers and school administrators who currently work in public schools.

Most educators working in public schools have less than twenty-five years of experience as certified teachers or administrators in the system (National Center for Education Statistics [NCES], 2013). Hence, the majority of teachers and school leaders have been professionally raised in a structure that knows nothing but standards and testing. There is little institutional or professional memory of life without performance/output-guarantee curriculum standards because much of that history has been removed from many teacher and school administrator preparation programs. The intellectual history of the system has been cleansed of notions that contradict the standardized marketing slogans.

Argument

This book argues, with data and evidence, that the assumptions underlying the need to standardize curriculum expectations and the claims of the effectives of standardization are fatally flawed. The book presents an alternative vision of what public school curriculum can be: A vision based on evidence and rooted in the ideas of child-centered, passion-based, locally controlled education. It is a vision to become unstandardized, diversified, and creative in the approach to curriculum design, development, implementation, and outputs.

Unstandardizing curricula, or diversifying curriculum expectations and learning experiences, includes a focus on skills and dispositions that transcend time and subject matter. Some, like state department of education bureaucrats, have termed such skills "21st-Century Skills" (e.g., New Jersey Department of Education [NJDOE], 2015). Skills commonly included as 21st century by state education bureaucrats include critical thinking, using technology to enhance productivity, planning education and career paths, research skills, and working productively in teams. Education bureaucrats commonly associate these skills solely with economic functions of public education: career training.

Unstandardized skills and dispositions go beyond those associated with economics and include things critical for socio-civic and avocational development of human beings. Economic output is a narrow interpretation of effective human development and a myopic view of the purposes of public education. To be unstandardized is to be a well-rounded, diversified human being and not just a tool for economic use. Although traditional twenty-first-century skills and dispositions are included in an unstandardized approach to curriculum design, development, and implementation, they are operationalized in diverse ways, so as to address multiple functions of public education and foster the development of well-rounded human beings.

Reflections in the Mirror

Those with more than twenty-five years' experience in education can probably remember a time when there were less state education curriculum standards and standardized testing. Some educators who began their careers before 1994 probably remember not having state-mandated content standards. Thus, those educators were not programmed to think that one-size-fits-all performance-guarantee curriculum standards, distally developed by bureaucrats and corporations, were the great equalizer for the achievement differences that existed among students.

Curriculum standards were developed locally and assessment decisions were also made locally in the majority of states prior to 1994. Prior to 1994 teachers created curriculum objectives and activities locally and customized them while planning lessons and teaching so as to better meet the needs of their local students. Parents, community members, and educators had more opportunities to influence curriculum standards and the curriculum of individual courses through a democratic process of strategic planning and local board of education meetings.

The standards and corresponding curriculum that grew from local strategic planning and board of education meetings were designed to nurture the children in the system. It was the opposite of designing a precast system and expecting all children to serve it. Many communities started with the question "What do we want for our children in the future?" This question led to the development of broad statements that today might be labeled Whole Child goals that addressed cognitive, social, and emotional growth.

The goals became the basis for specific grade-level curricula development via learning objectives, activities, and assessments. The grade-level curricula gave way to customized activities within the individual schools and classrooms by the teachers. Curricular customization was not an add-on. It was an expectation, as was customized teaching. The act of teaching was about making the curriculum fit the students within your class. Students were not viewed as deficient square pegs that needed to be reshaped into circles all with the same circumference.

Prior to the era of mass standardization educators could not give excuses such as, "Well the Common Core requires us to . . ." whenever a parent came to request a change in the way educators worked with his/her child. The superintendent could not use Smarter Balanced Assessment Consortium (SBAC) or Partnership for the Assessment of Readiness for College and Careers (PARCC) requirements as a way to dodge parent or community members' requests for more input into program changes or more complex and creative coursework.

Superintendents could not use standardization as a lever to coerce or pressure teachers to mechanize practices to align with a state paperwork mandate. Principals could not hide behind a corporately produced curriculum to avoid dealing with a parental request for better education of his or her child. Prior to mass standardization educators felt the pressures of a professional democracy that required customization. The students, community, parents and guardians, the principal, and colleagues all had expectations.

During those times many educators used the term "well rounded" to describe the social, emotional, cognitive, socio-civic, and vocational goals that became the foundation for curriculum design and development (Tanner and Tanner, 2007). The broad goals that inspired the macro-curriculum, or school-wide programs bubbled up from the grassroots as much as they poured down from the school district central office. Goals were rarely sent as directives from elites working in offices far away from the town and children.

This is not to say that there were not disagreements within school districts. There were many and they occurred often. Democracy is messy. It's not efficient. But it is within that democratic messiness that blossomed ideas and expectations that marinated and eventually became programs that addressed more needs of more children. It is important to remember that public school is first and foremost the incubator of democracy, and thus, life-impacting decisions about children and education personnel must be made through democratic processes, such as strategic planning and public meetings, and that takes time (Dewey, 1916).

Not every school district engages the full community in democratic strategic planning. Not all school district leaders allow for maximum democratic community engagement and input at meetings. In fact, some school district leaders try to stifle input, engagement, and the overall democratic process. They try to hide behind their titles and state edicts so as to surrender decision-making and responsibility. They are not education leaders. They are puppets of bad policy.

Standardization and authoritarianism are generally more efficient and easier for those who occupy positions of power than the hard work of customization and nurturing democracy. Perhaps that is one reason the authoritarian use of one-size-fits-all curriculum standards and testing have become so entrenched in public school education reform. It is easier to issue edicts to the public than to engage and collaborate with them. How did public education arrive at a place where the student must fit a standardized system developed far from the lives of actual children?

Forward, March!

Frederick Taylor's (1947) Scientific Management principles propelled standardization into the mainstream of American life. Books like Arthur Bestor's (1985) *Educational Wastelands* further fanned the flames for increasing amounts of standardization in public schools. The promises of effectiveness brought forth by Taylor (1947) and doubts cast on the public system by *Wastelands* were connected with Sputnik I and what Don Orlich and I cited as the genesis of the modern school reform standardization movement (Tienken and Orlich, 2013). The momentum for standardization created by the Sputnik launches lasted through most of the 1960s and then moderated somewhat, until the 1983 release of *A Nation at Risk* (National Commission on Excellence in Education [NCEE], 1983) and Wastelands in 1985.

The steady march toward mass homogenization of curriculum standards and academic proficiency testing has proceeded relatively unabated since the Reagan administration's release of *A Nation at Risk* unleashed the "rising tide of mediocrity" upon the public school system (NCEE, 1983, p. 6). The authors of *A Nation at Risk* (NCEE, 1983) cited general trends from results of international tests to support recommendations based on standardized performance goals such as (a) the coursework required to earn a high school diploma, (b) standardized competency testing at transition points within the K–12 system, (c) teacher preparation and employment, and (d) the amount of time spent in school.

Bankrupt Ideas

Although thoroughly debunked first in the *Sandia Report* (Carson, Huelskamp, and Woodall, 1993), and later by other researchers (e.g., Bracey, 1999; Berliner and Biddle, 1995), some education bureaucrats and policy makers continue to unknowingly or unscrupulously reference the educationally bankrupt report to justify their support of the latest iteration of a standardized program being foisted upon the over 56 million public school children in the United States. Sandia pierced the veil of lies but few educators currently working have ever read it.

Risk reintroduced the American public to the enchantment of the traditional essentialist conception of curriculum as something developed by others, for teachers to deliver to waiting students as part of the act of knowledge transmission. It also reignited the connection between education and economic national security so well developed by the propaganda surrounding the Soviet's launch of Sputnik. It is a traditionalist conception of curriculum and the fear of future economic insecurity that fuels the current passion for standardization in education reform policies.

The promise of the standardization of outputs, the universal performance-guarantee if you will, measured by standardized instruments, to secure an economic future for all children in America is an alluring and recurring argument used by successive presidential administrations and self-anointed education reformers. The would-be reformers pound on the drums of global competitiveness and lagging student achievement compared to international peers in order to inject ever-increasing amounts of standardization into the public system. *Risk* was the booster-shot the education reform community needed after the initial Sputnik injection to infect the entire public school system with the standardized snake oil.

Into the Bushes We Go

The public school crisis momentum created by *Risk* during the Reagan administration hurtled itself into the Bush I administration and resulted in a clarion call on September 28, 1989, by the president for "national performance goals" (Bush, 1989). President George H. W. Bush issued a joint statement at the conclusion of the Charlottesville Education Summit. The president declared:

> Education has always been important, but never this important because the stakes have changed: Our competitors for opportunity are also working to educate their people. As they continue to improve, they make the future a moving target. We believe that the time has come, for the first time in U.S. history, to establish clear, national performance goals, goals that will make us internationally competitive.

Just as presidents before him had done, George H. W. Bush used his statement to draw a straight line that connected performance-guarantee standards to economic security and national security through an increasing use of the doctrine of specificity. The president went on to describe seven areas that national performance goals should address:

> By performance we mean goals that will, if achieved, guarantee that we are internationally competitive, such as goals related to: (a) the readiness of children to start school; (b) the performance of students on international achievement tests, especially in math and science; (c) the reduction of the dropout rate and the improvement of academic performance, especially among at-risk students; (d) the functional literacy of adult Americans; (e) the level of training necessary to guarantee a competitive workforce; (f) the supply of qualified teachers and up-to-date technology; and (g) the establishment of safe, disciplined, and drug-free schools.

The seven areas identified by Bush at the Education Summit eventually become a centerpiece of the president's State of the Union address on January 31, 1990. By then, the areas had morphed into six specific goals to be achieved by 2000 (Bush, 1990):

- By the year 2000, every child must start school ready to learn.
- The United States must increase the high school graduation rate to no less than 90 percent. And we are going to make sure our schools' diplomas mean something. In critical subjects at the 4th, 8th, and 12th grades we must assess our students' performance.
- By the year 2000, U.S. students must be first in the world in math and science achievement.
- Every American adult must be a skilled, literate worker and citizen.
- Every school must offer the kind of disciplined environment that makes it possible for our kids to learn.
- And every school in America must be drug-free.

Clearly, the race was on to standardize the performance of America's public school children and national standards were going to play a part. George H. W. Bush was able to elevate the ideas presented in *Risk* into specific goals that could eventually be legislated. With that legislation would come a historic change in the philosophy that would drive future education reform; a philosophical shift from local control to centralized bureaucracy and decision-making.

Goals2000 Educate America

Almost exactly four years after President George H. W. Bush presented the national performance goals to the American public in his 1990 State of the Union Address, the U.S. Congress passed, and President Bill Clinton signed into law, the Goals2000 Educate America Act (P.L. 103–227). Clinton's signature on the bill made the six original goals put forward by President George H.W. Bush law along with two more goals added to the bill:

> The nation's teaching force will have access to programs for the continued improvement of their professional skills and the opportunity to acquire the knowledge and skills needed to instruct and prepare all American students for the next century. Every school will promote partnerships that will increase parental involvement and participation in promoting the social, emotional, and academic growth of children.

The bill also expanded upon the original recommendation for testing in grades 4, 8, and 12 by adding the word *competency* and it identified specific subjects in which students should demonstrate competency, as measured by standardized test results, partially to ensure productive employment in the future (P.L. 103–227):

> All students will leave grades 4, 8, and 12 having demonstrated competency over challenging subject matter including English, mathematics, science, foreign languages, civics and government, economics, the arts, history, and geography, and every school in America will ensure that all students learn to use their minds well, so they may be prepared for responsible citizenship, further learning, and productive employment in our nation's modern economy.

The die was cast for the later rollout of college and career readiness under the banner of competency. The word *competency* was central to the shift in the way education policy would be shaped going forward. *Competency* would help to add some teeth and bite to the prevailing standardized conception of curriculum. The addition of just one word, "competency," solidified the focus on outputs and performance of schooling that dominates the education policy environment today.

Competency replaced equity and equality of inputs, resources and access to quality. As long as children and educators were competent in the identified goals, nothing else mattered. Demonstrating competency was all about output, regardless of input. Input was no longer relevant. Thus, inequalities of inputs that were baked into the system via increasing poverty and other social problems that directly affect academic output on standardized tests became invisible in policy-making circles. Poof, it's magic!

President Clinton continued the education-economic narrative established by his predecessors as he stumped for passage of Goals2000 in 1993. He argued for the need to pass his education bill on economic grounds in front of members of the National Education Association at their annual meeting in San Francisco:

> We can make sure that our students lead the world in math and science achievement. We can make sure that we can compete in the global economy and live in the global village. As I head overseas, I'm reminded how much more we need to do.

Clinton's focus on output guarantee paved the way for standardization of student performance and instructional processes to replace equity of inputs and resources. The infatuation with standardization would eventually turn the Elementary and Secondary Education Act into a weapon of mass destruction against local control, creative curriculum development, and a democratic public school system. The weapon became known as No Child Left Behind (NCLB) (Tienken and Orlich, 2013).

Educating Under the Influence

Of course some state departments of education developed state curriculum standards and testing in some or all subject areas prior Clinton's signing of the 1994 law. For example, New York had the Regents Exams for decades before Goals2000. But Goals2000 was a marked turning point from a philosophy of input guarantee, in which funding for schools through the Elementary and Secondary Education Act primarily focused on ensuring that school students had more equal inputs in terms of resources, to an output-guarantee philosophy in which competency and standardized performance expectations became king.

Performance-guarantee policies seek to equalize performance expectations for all students in aggregate and in subgroups. For example, the performance outputs for students with special needs are identical to those for students without such needs. Policy makers and education reformers who operate under the influence of performance-guarantee ideology believe it is a lack of high expectations that is maintaining the achievement differences on standardized tests, not a difference in inputs and resources. They believe that by standardizing performance expectations and standardizing the system in which those expectations are extracted, all students will achieve at similar levels, regardless of inputs.

Policy makers under the influence of performance-guarantee ideology measure progress toward standardized outcomes through results from standardized testing. Goals2000 represented the national adoption of the performance-guarantee ideology and the idol-worship of standardized curriculum expectations and testing to achieve the aims of the policies built on the ideology. Some form of unstandardized rehabilitation is certainly in order.

New Jersey under the Influence

Those educators working in New Jersey prior to 1995 lived through the transformation from an input-guarantee system to the output-guarantee environment that exists. The original set of New Jersey Core Curriculum Content Standards (NJCCCS) and state mandated standardized tests were imposed by former Governor Christine Todd Whitman as part of a public school funding lawsuit her administration lost, known as *Abbott v. Burke*. Her administration was charged by the court with determining how much a "thorough and efficient" education would cost in New Jersey to meet the resource input mandates in the Comprehensive Educational Improvement and Financing Act (known as CEIFA). The CEIFA was New Jersey's latest iteration of a school funding formula in which school districts located in New Jersey's poorest communities argued that their children were being short-changed in terms of the inputs necessary to provide their children with an effective education.

Attorneys for the school districts made arguments from an input-guarantee viewpoint, whereas the state offered arguments more closely aligned with a performance-guarantee ideology. The school districts won the cases, but the Whitman administration, and champions of the performance-guarantee ideology, ultimately won the war.

In order to determine the per-pupil cost of a "thorough and efficient" education, Whitman tasked the NJDOE with creating a set of curriculum performance standards to define the "thorough and efficient" mandate in the state constitution. After the performance standards were developed, Whitman's administration put a price tag on education in New Jersey to support her suggested state funding levels and demonstrate to the court that she was funding schools in good faith and in line with the funding formula.

Without physically being in the room when then original set of New Jersey standards were being developed requires one to conjecture about the ultimate goal of Whitman's plan. But it is not beyond the realm of possibility to suggest that the plan was not to develop the most expansive and highest quality standards possible. The goal was to lower the per-pupil cost of education so that the state was responsible for less of the funding. This conjecture is supported.

Thus, New Jersey's first set of mandated performance-based curriculum standards and high stakes tests were created to satisfy legal, economic, and political mandates, not for reasons of education quality. The Whitman administration was off the funding hook, so to speak, but New Jersey's public school children were thrown into a standardized system that would later lead to greater loss of local control and bureaucratic micromanagement and mismanagement of curricula, instruction, and assessment.

But the creation of the NJCCCS also satisfied another objective. Their creation marked a turning point in state school funding and accountability methods. The NJDOE bureaucrats and some sympathetic state legislators were able to redirect the input-guarantee argument away from the singular focus on equalized inputs and toward equalized outputs. They built the foundation for arguing against making monetary decisions based on the need for equitable inputs and instead created the basis for advocating in favor of standardized performance targets and measures regardless of the diverse needs of students around the state.

The strategy of using the argument of one's opponent to achieve one's objectives is reminiscent of the magician who draws the eyes of his audience to the fact that there is "nothing in the hat" but then pulls an ace out of his sleeve while the audience looks at the hat. Abracadabra, you are now in a performance-guarantee, standardized system.

Back to the Future

The original set of NJ state standards and assessments launched in 1997, and created for economic and political purposes, were later used by another regime of standardization proponents to legitimize the 2010 installation of the Common Core State Standards (CCSS) and PARCC testing in the state. Ironically, those original standards and standardized tests so heavily touted by earlier legions of NJDOE bureaucrats and their governors, were later deemed ineffective and of low quality by a new education reform crew housed in the NJDOE in 2010. One standardized solution was then substituted for another in a game of "my brand of standardization is better than yours."

This standardized bait and switch routine happened all around the country. State education agency bureaucrats from California to New York vilified their state's original sets of performance standards and tests, even though they had used them to judge the quality of teachers and school districts for the prior decade. Those original sets of performance standards and tests became persona non grata in favor of the newest standardized flavor of the week, Common Core and national standardized tests SBAC and PARCC.

Actually, this entire "new and improved" system of standardization and testing is reminiscent of something tried in this country over 100 years ago: the Lancasterian system. The Lancasterian system of education was based on the factory model of standardizing, mechanizing, monitoring, and lowering the cost of education. The standardized Lancasterin system failed miserably and those who supported it are the butt of jokes in the curriculum research community. The idea rests near the top of the heap of failed reforms aimed at bringing greater efficiencies to public education.

No Child Left Behind

The logical evolution of Goals2000 was the NCLB Act (NCLB, 2002, 115 STAT. 1425). Although Goals2000 triggered funding for states to support the development of performance standards and testing to monitor performance, it lacked the teeth that some education reformers wanted to see bite into the public school system. Enter President George W. Bush and his psychometric vision of education reform.

Bush explained his vision at the National Association for the Advancement of Colored People (NAACP) 91st annual conference when he was still candidate George W. Bush.

> Under my vision, all students must be measured. We must test to know. And low-performing schools, those schools that won't teach and won't change, will have three years to produce results, three years to meet standards, three years to make sure the very faces of our future are not mired in mediocrity. And if they're not able to do so, the resources must go to the parents so that parents can make a different choice. You see, no child, no child should be left behind in America. (Bush, 2000).

George W. Bush's vision became the NCLB Act of 2001, signed on January 8, 2002. But at the end of the day, the NCLB Act was the natural evolution of Goals2000 and the bonding of the performance-guarantee vision to public school education reform policy making. The various accountability mandates within the NCLB Act illustrate the construction of a standardization framework that was meant to penetrate the depths of the locally controlled public school system (NCLB, 2002, 115 STAT. 1425). The multiple layers of performance-guarantee standardization built into the Act and the reliance on data from standardized measures to judge school personnel were unprecedented, but not a surprise given the consistent evolution of standardized policy making.

Some of the more salient features of the standardization framework required (a) standardized academic content and student achievement standards for each state (Sec. 1111.b.1.A–F); (b) all students tested in mathematics and reading/language arts in grades 3 through 8 and one time in high school (Sec. 1111.b.1.A–F; Sec. 1111b.3.A–C); (c) separate measures to be reported for (1) all K–12 children, (2) the economically disadvantaged, (3) students from major racial and ethnic groups, (4) students with disabilities, and (5) students with limited English proficiency (Sec.1111.b.2.A–K); (d) mandated use of public tax dollars to pay private tutoring corporations for supplemental educational services (SES) programs for students in schools deemed as in need of improvement based on the results from the yearly mandated tests (Sec. 1114.b.8.A); and (e) automatic triggers that provide for school takeovers and outsourcing to charter schools or other corporately supported entities regardless of local governance decisions to the contrary (Sec. 1114.b.8.A–C).

The teeth of the act were seen in the coupling of standardization of curriculum expectations and assessments, performance measures, and outsourcing of public school functions to the private sector. But George W. Bush's vision was not all that original. In fact, it was very similar to the vision of education put forth in 1978 with the release of the report *Improving Educational Achievement* (Committee on Testing and Basic Skills, 1978).

The authors of the 1978 report advocated for reforms to public schools and recommended a full return to "Basic Skills" in order to improve education for all students. The authors championed test-based accountability for teachers and school administrators and proposed that increased achievement-test scores should be a goal of government. Looking back at Goals2000, one can see also the influence of the somewhat unknown report with its focus on language arts and mathematics achievement and a singular focus on teacher quality over sociological issues such as poverty.

The 1978 Committee on Testing and Basic Skills authors argued for the need to improve teacher quality as a way to improve student performance. The ideology of performance-based guarantee is embedded in the report. Tienken and Orlich (2013) were so struck by the similarities of the recommendations made in the 1978 report to those eventually incorporated into the NCLB Act that the authors wrote:

> "Several statements seem prophetic now. American education should be paying much more attention to doing a thorough job in the fundamentals of reading, writing, and arithmetic…" (p. iii). "Tests can play several different roles. One is as a means of public accountability…" (p. 7). It seems as though the underlying concepts of NCLB have been around for quite some time. (Tienken and Orlich, 2013, p. 54)

The underlying linear framework woven through the NCLB Act and most education reform policies that rest upon standardization is generally extorted from very primitive rationalist and behaviorist theories of education. Those theories fit snuggly with the traditionalist conception of curriculum. The enforcement end of most standardization policies are operationalized via use of positive reinforcement and negative reinforcement, known idiomatically as the carrots and sticks approach (Andreoni, Harbaugh, and Versterlund, 2003; Tienken, 2016). Bryk and Hermanson (1993) identified the approach as an "instrumental use" model of policy making (p. 453). The NCLB Act made full use of the instrumental use model and instrumental use describes Bush's vision very well.

The seductive and easy-to-understand sequence inherent within instrumental use models is that a policy body, like the U.S. Congress or state legislature, develops a set of desired performance outcomes or guarantees, monitors the relationship between the outcomes and school processes through structures like school rating schemes linked to state-mandated standardized test results, and then implements a series of punishments or rewards aimed to change behavior to align with the policy-making vision (Baker, Oluwole, and Green, 2013). The instrumental use vision relies heavily on the unquestioning belief that the test results from state-mandated assessments are meaningful indicators of output.

Advocates of using results from standardized tests to judge the quality of the implementation of the standardized policies proclaim, without empirical evidence, that the use of results from state standardized tests in overtly public ways causes students and teachers to work harder and achieve higher levels of the intended outcome because the tests create teaching and learning targets that have perceived meanings to both groups (Reed, Scull, Slicker, and Northern, 2012).

Those same core aspects of performance-guarantee standardization, enforced with standardized testing found in the 1978 report *Improving Educational Achievement* (Committee on Testing and Basic Skills, 1978) and *A Nation at Risk* (NCEE, 1983), continue to be seen in more recent policies and programs that apply standardization and incremental use theories to guide policy making.

Marching Along to the Common Core State Standards

The logical next step down the performance-guarantee rabbit hole was the adoption of a common set of curriculum standards across states. One of the main criticisms raised by proponents of standardization against NCLB was that it created fifty different sets of expectations, via the development of fifty sets of state standards (e.g., Carmichael, Wilson, Porter-Magee, and Martino, 2010; Conley, Drummond, de Gonzalez, Rooseboom, and Stout, 2011). The CCSS were a highly touted solution to the perceived lack of standardization of curriculum standards and testing proliferated by the NCLB Act.

Essentially, one argument made by proponents for Common Core was that NCLB Act did not mandate enough standardization among state standards and standardized assessments. The development of the CCSS allowed states to adopt a curricular product, a copyrighted common set of standards for mathematics and language arts and purchase or create tests aligned to those common standards. As of 2016 more than forty states have done so.

According to the purveyors of the CCSS (National Governors Association and Council of Chief State School Officers [NGA and CCSSO], 2015) the standards fix the problems associated with the standardization policies of the NCLB era created by fifty different sets of standards and ensure that all students will be ready for college and careers and be able to out-compete their international peers.

> High standards that are consistent across states provide teachers, parents, and students with a set of clear expectations to ensure that all students have the skills and knowledge necessary to succeed in college, career, and life upon graduation from high school, regardless of where they live. These standards are aligned to the expectations of colleges, workforce training programs, and employers. The standards promote equity by ensuring all students are well prepared to collaborate and compete with their peers in the United States and abroad.

The vendors of the CCSS address equity through performance-guarantee; the subtle bigotry of standardized expectations. The root causes of under-achievement are swept aside as excuses made by lazy teachers, students, and parents.

Although the CCSS have been marketed and sold to the American public as a silver bullet, "state-led initiative" (NGA and CCSSO, 2015), developed by experts and teachers from around the country, their roots sprout from the corporate world, with one of the main players being standardization advocate Achieve, Inc.

Achieve, Inc. was created by the NGA, a private organization, and various business leaders from some of the nation's largest corporations in 1996, during the National Education Summit held by President Bill Clinton (Achieve, Inc., 2004a). Clinton viewed the corporate world as an ally to operationalize the full power of the vision of Goals2000. Clinton opened the doors of the United States Department of Education (USDOE) to the corporate world in hopes of improving education for all children.

By 2004, Achieve, Inc., along with standardization supporters like the Education Trust and the Thomas B. Fordham Institute, released the report *Ready or Not: Creating a High School Diploma that Counts* and simultaneously launched the American Diploma Project (ADP), which some identified as the forerunner to the CCSS (Achieve, Inc., 2004b; Vander Hart, 2014). Many of the requirements listed in the ADP found a home in the forthcoming Race to the Top competitive grant program and CCSS.

Teachers Need Not Apply

Far from being an open and democratic process of creation, Karp (2013) captured the essence of the main participants of the final versions of the CCSS when he exposed that "the standards were drafted largely behind closed doors by academics and assessment 'experts,' many with ties to testing companies" (p. 13). Cody (2013) found similar undemocratic links between the development of CCSS and the corporate world:

> A "confidential" process was under way, involving 27 people on two Work Groups, including a significant number from the testing industry. Here are the affiliations of those 27: ACT (6), the College Board (6), Achieve Inc. (8), Student Achievement Partners (2), America's Choice (2). Only three participants were outside of these five organizations. ONLY ONE classroom teacher WAS involved—on the committee to review the math standards. (p. 1)

Karp (2013) and Cody (2013) noted that not one of the participants on the standards development committees represented the K–3 teaching spectrum and K–12 educators were brought into the process at the end to act as a rubber stamp and endorse the privately developed standards. Evidence-based voices that questioned standardization were not represented on the development committees. The lack of K–12 educator input into the actual development of the Standards is perhaps paled in comparison only by the amount of private money used to market the standards. For example, the Gates Foundation reportedly has spent over 160 million dollars as of 2013 to promote the Common Core, with other smaller foundations spending funds to do the same (Simon and Shah, 2013).

The NCLB Act was so unpopular by the time President Obama entered office in 2009 that he had to put forth some type of change that could occur without an act of Congress. Because Congress was not going to take up reauthorization of the NCLB Act early in the president's first term, that precluded any large-scale education policy initiatives coming via legislation. However, Obama was able to secure funding for an education grant program administered by the USDOE. That grant program became known as "Race to the Top" (NGA and CCSSO, 2015).

STANDARDIZED ASSUMPTIONS

The current disciples of common curriculum standards proselytize standardization via a set of assumptions. First, they proclaim that achievement of students in America's public school lag woefully behind the achievement of students in other countries. The disciples point to ranks of U.S. students on international tests of academic achievement for the quantitative data they need to support their claim. Next, proponents of standardization warn that the economic future of the United States and global economic competitiveness of public school children rely on outranking students from other nations on international tests. Finally, they present the solution: Standardized expectations for curricula, assessment, and instructional methods. The assumptions allow for simplistic, ready-made solutions.

President Obama used the standardized assumption to forward his administration's education agenda. Obama maintained the tradition of connecting economic security to education reform in his introductory remarks about the Race to the Top program:

> In an economy where knowledge is the most valuable commodity a person and a country have to offer, the best jobs will go to the best educated, whether they live in the United States or India or China. In a world where countries that out-educate us today will out-compete us tomorrow, the future belongs to the nation that best educates its people. Period. We know this.

Period! It's that simple. Obama defined the problem simplistically as a lagging of academic performance on the part of U.S. public school students compared to international peers. Next he presented the ready-made solution through a performance-guarantee scheme:

> And one of the benchmarks we will use is whether states are designing and enforcing higher and clearer standards and assessments that prepare a student to graduate from college and succeed in life.

The solution is simple: fix the lag and solve the dual crises of student achievement concerns and economic security. The rabbit appears out of the hat yet again. In Obama's education vision, the benchmarks that he referred to were the guaranteed outputs in the form of standardized tests results that he believes predict college and career readiness. Although little is known about how the president defines "succeed in life," one is left to infer that higher tests scores on international tests of academic knowledge and national tests aligned to so-called college and career ready standards are the proxies to predict future success for the over 50 million students that attend public schools.

It all sounds so easy. Start with a performance-guarantee philosophy. Next add some instrumental use theory. Then, bake-in heavy doses of standardization to the junk-science mixture. Finally, wait about thirteen years for the student to finish K–12 schooling, and poof, success in college and careers. Just follow the recipe. Who wouldn't agree with that logical and foolproof process?

NEXT STEPS

The rhetoric supporting standardization practices rests wholly or in large part on the overt or implied connection between education and economic competitiveness. President Obama was just another bureaucrat in a long line of policy makers who followed the flawed ideology of standardization since the Soviet launch of *Sputnik 1* (Tienken and Orlich, 2013). As the most recent election cycle has demonstrated, Obama is certainly not the last to bite the poison apple. Many policy makers and educators have been infected.

Is there a cause-and-effect connection between education output and economic security, especially as measured by international tests that support the arguments for standardization? The next chapter will challenge one of the most important precepts of the standardized performance-guarantee system: Achievement data from international tests are important barometers of student output and those data should guide judgments made about education reform policies. The next chapter presents an argument, with evidence, that the results on international tests do not matter, and that making education policy decisions based on the results is education malpractice.

REFERENCES

Achieve, Inc. (2004a). *Our history*. Washington, DC: Achieve, Inc. Retrieved from http://www.achieve.org/history-achieve.

Achieve, Inc. (2004b). *The American diploma project. Ready or not: Creating a high school diploma that counts*. Washington, DC: Achieve, Inc. Retrieved from http://www.achieve.org/files/ReadyorNot.pdf.

Andreoni, J., Harbaugh, W., & Vesterlund, L. (2003). The carrot or the stick: Rewards, punishments, and cooperation. *American Economic Review*, 93(3), 893–902.

Baker, B.D., Oluwole, J., & Green, P. C. III. (2013). The legal consequences of mandating high stakes decisions based on low quality information: Teacher evaluation in the race-to-the-top era. *Education Policy Analysis Archives, 21*(5).

Berliner, D.C. & Biddle, B.J. (1995). *The manufactured crisis: Myths, frauds and the attack on America's public schools*. Reading, MA: Addison-Wesley.

Bestor, A. (1985). *Educational wastelands: The retreat from learning in our public schools* (2nd ed.). Urbana: University of Illinois Press.

Bracey, G. (1999). The propaganda of "A Nation at Risk." Retrieved from http://www.america-tomorrow.com/bracey/EDDRA/EDDRA8.htm.

Bredo, E. (2002). The Darwinian center to the vision of William James. In J. Garrison, P. Poedeschi, & E. Bredo (Eds.), *William James and education*. New York: Teachers College Press.

Bryk, A. & Hermanson, K. (1993). Educational indicator systems: Observations on their structure, interpretation and use. In L. Darling-Hammond (Ed.), *Review of*

Research in Education, 19 (pp. 451–484). Washington, DC: American Educational Research Association.

Bush, G.W. (2000, July 10). George W. Bush's speech to the NAACP. *Washington Post.* Retrieved from http://www.washingtonpost.com/wp-srv/onpolitics/elections/bushtext071000.htm.

Bush, G.H.W. (1989, September 28). *Joint statement on the education summit with the nation's governors in Charlottesville, Virginia.* Retrieved from http://www.presidency.ucsb.edu/ws/?pid=17580.

Bush, G.H.W. (1990, January 31). *Address before a joint session of the congress on the state of the union.* Retrieved from http://www.presidency.ucsb.edu/ws/?pid=18095.

Callahan, R.E. (1962). *The cult of efficiency.* Chicago: The University of Chicago Press.

Carmichael, S.B., Wilson, W.S., Porter-Magee, K., & Martino, G. (2010). *The state of state standards and the Common Core in 2010.* Washington, DC: The Thomas B. Fordham Institute. Retrieved from http://www.edexcellence.net/publications/the-state-of-state-of-standards-and-the-common-core-in-2010.html.

Carson, C.C., Huelskamp, R.M., & Woodall, T.D. (1993, May/June). Perspectives on education in America: An annotated briefing [known as the Sandia Report]. *Journal of Educational Research, 86*(5), 259–310.

Clinton, W.J. (1993, July 5). *Remarks to the National Education Association in San Francisco, California.* Retrieved from http://www.presidency.ucsb.edu/ws/index.php?pid=46808.

Cody, A. (2013, November 16). *Common core standards: 10 colossal errors.* Living in Dialogue. Retrieved from http://blogs.edweek.org/teachers/living-in-dialogue/2013/11/common_core_standards_ten_colo.html.

Committee on Testing and Basic Skills. (1978). *Improving educational achievement.* Washington, DC: National Academy of Education.

Conley, D.T., Drummond, K.V., de Gonzalez, A., Rooseboom, J., & Stout. O. (2011). *Lining up: The relationship between the common core State standards and five sets of comparison standards.* Eugene, OR: Educational Policy Improvement Center.

Dewey, J. (1902). *The child and the curriculum.* Chicago: The University of Chicago Press.

Dewey, J. (1916). *Democracy and education.* New York: McMillan.

Dewey, J. (1929) *Sources of science in education.* New York: Liveright.

Duncan, A. (2012, December 11). *Statement by U.S. secretary of education arne Duncan on the release of the 2011 TIMSS and PIRLS assessments.* Retrieved from http://www.ed.gov/news/press-releases/statement-us-secretary-education-arne-duncan-release-2011-timss-and-pirls-assess.

Duncan, A. (2013, December 3). *The threat of educational stagnation and complacency.* Retrieved from http://www.ed.gov/news/speeches/threat-educational-stagnation-and-complacency.

Freier, P. (2000). Pedagogy of the oppressed: 30th anniversary edition. New York: Continuum.

Goals2000 Educate America Act, Pub. L. No. 103–227, 108 Stat. 125. (1994). Retrieved from http://www2.ed.gov/legislation/GOALS2000/TheAct/index.html.

Karp, S. (2013). The problems with the Common Core. *Rethinking Schools, 28*(2), 10–17.

Mann, H. (1848). *Twelfth annual report of the board of education together with the twelfth annual report of the secretary of the board.* Boston, Massachusetts: Dutton and Wentworth State Printers.

National Center for Education Statistics. (2013). Schools and Staffing Survey (SASS), Public School Teacher Data File, 2011–12. Author. Retrieved from https://nces.ed.gov/programs/digest/d13/tables/dt13_209.30.asp.

National Commission on Excellence in Education. (1983). *A nation at risk.* Washington, DC: U.S. Department of Education.

National Governors Association and Council of Chief State School Officers. (2015). *Common core state standards: Frequently asked questions.* Washington, DC: NGA and CCSSO. Retrieved from http://www.corestandards.org/about-the-standards/frequently-asked-questions/#faq-2309.

New Jersey Department of Education. (2015). *Career ready practices.* Author. Retrieved from http://www.state.nj.us/education/cte/hl/CRP.pdf.

No Child Left Behind (NCLB) Act of 2001, Pub. L. No. 107–110, § 115, Stat. 1425. (2002).

Obama, B. (2009, July 24). *Remarks by the President on education.* The Whitehouse. Retrieved from https://www.whitehouse.gov/the_press_office/Remarks-by-the-President-at-the-Department-of-Education/.

Rao, M.H.S. & Bargerstock, A. (2011). Exploring the role of standard costing in lean manufacturing enterprises: A structuration theory approach. *Management Accounting Quarterly, 13*(1), 47–60.

Rayman, R. (1981). Joseph Lancaster's monitorial system of education and American Indian education. *History of Education Quarterly, 21*(4), 395–409.

Reed, E., Scull, J., Slicker, G., & Winkler, A. M. (2012). *Defining strong state accountability systems: How can better standards gain greater traction? A first look.* Washington, DC: Thomas B. Fordham Institute.

Simon, S. & Shah, N. (2013, September 9). The common core money war. *Politico.* Retrieved from http://www.politico.com/story/2013/09/education-common-core-standards-schools-096964#ixzz2fkL8jstZ.

Tanner, D. & Tanner, L. (2007). *Curriculum development: Theory into practice.* Upper Saddle River, NJ: Pearson.

Taylor, F.W. (1947). *Scientific management.* New York: Harper and Brothers.

Thorndike, E.L. (1924). Mental discipline in high school studies. *Journal of Educational Psychology, 15*: 1–22, 98.

Tienken, C.H. (2016). Standardized test results can be predicted, so stop using them to drive education policymaking. In C. Tienken & C. Mullen (Eds.), *Education policy perils: Tackling the tough issues* (pp. 157–185). Philadelphia, PA: Taylor Francis Routledge.

Tienken, C.H. & Orlich, D.C. (2013). *The school reform landscape: Fraud, myth, and lies.* New York, NY: Rowman and Littlefield.

Tramaglini, T.W. & Tienken, C.H. (2016). Customized curriculum and high achievement in high poverty schools. In C. Tienken & C. Mullen (Eds.), *Education policy perils: Tackling the tough issues* (pp. 75–101). Philadelphia, PA: Taylor Francis.

Vander Hart, S. (2014). Common Core: The silent revolution in education policy. In Lombard (Ed.), *Common ground on Common Core*, 3–18. Madison, WI: Resounding Books.

Chapter 2

The Competitiveness Hoax

There is no doubt that the academic achievement of U.S. public school students, as a group, lags behind students in most of the industrialized world when measured by rankings on international tests. The claims by education pundits and proponents of standardization that U.S. students do not rank at the top of the world in mathematics, reading, and science are correct. But if the overall fate of the country relied on U.S. students ranking high on international tests, then we should all be reciting a different version of the Pledge of Allegiance by now. But that is not the case.

The fact that U.S. rankings on international tests have not caused the economic or political collapse of the nation has not stopped proponents of standardization from using the rankings to incite fear and uncertainty over a lack of global competitiveness and national security. In turn, the fear and uncertainty are used to drive education policy proposals aimed at standardizing the U.S. public school system. For example, marketing materials related to the "Race to the Top" grant program and the CCSS initiative cited global competitiveness and claims of lagging U.S. student achievement as some of the reasons for the need to impose mass standardization on the public school system.

History of Failure

As an aggregate group, students from the United States have never ranked particularly high on international tests. For example, 13-year-old students from the United States ranked 11th out of 12 countries on the First International Math Study (FIMS) of 1964, the first international test of mathematics administered. Several years later, 14-year-old students from the United States ranked seventh out of 14 countries on the First International Science Study (FISS) of 1970.

U.S. students continued their pattern of not ranking at the top of the world on the administration of the Second International Math Study (SIMS) in 1982.

U.S. students went on to rank 16th on the grade 8 mathematics portion of 1995 Third International Math and Science Study (TIMSS). U.S. students routinely rank in the middle of the pack, in the low 20s to low 30s, and around the international average score, on the Programme for International Student Assessment (PISA) administered to 15-year-olds in math, reading, and science. The aggregate scores for U.S. students generally do not rise higher than the middle of any international testing pack in any subject.

A Serious Case of PISA Envy

The rankings of U.S. students on international tests of academic skills and knowledge played an influential role in influencing performance-guarantee legislation and policies built on the foundations of standardization. Proponents of curriculum and assessment standardization policies often cite results from international tests or the goal of ranking first in the world on such tests to justify proposals to standardize processes and performance within the public school system.

President Obama's first Secretary of Education, Arne Duncan (2013), warned the nation that the entire U.S. public education system was in a state of dangerous stagnation and needed to follow the path of standardization set out by policies and programs associated with the CCSS and the Race to the Top grant program. Bureaucrats will continue to issue dire warnings of imminent economic collapse each time international test results, like those from PISA, are reported. International test results are the gifts that keep on giving proponents of standardization something to talk about and use to incite fear of education collapse.

PISA is an international assessment developed by the Organisation for Economic Co-operation and Development (OECD), a private international organization made up of 30 major industrialized countries and approximately 40 other partner countries and cities (OECD, 2013a.). A major focus of the OECD is the proliferation of privatization and free-market economic policies around the globe to improve global competitiveness. The OECD often recommends a series of privatization and neoliberal policies that benefit corporate interests over human interests. For example, the most frequent recommendations made by OECD are that countries should (a) privatize healthcare services; (b) add private competition to education systems and eliminate job security; (c) increase their unemployment rates in order to increase job insecurity to decrease wages; and (d) enter into free trade agreements that result in out-sourcing of jobs in order to keep consumer prices lower.

The OECD's interest in education rests upon its leadership's belief in a linear relationship between standardizing education output and future economic strength. Former Secretary of Education Arne Duncan (2012) asserted his perceived importance of PISA rankings following the release of the 2012 results:

> The PISA is an important, comparative snapshot of U.S. performance because the assessment is taken by 15-year-olds in high school around the globe. The big picture of U.S. performance on the 2012 PISA is straightforward and stark: It is a picture of educational stagnation. That brutal truth, that urgent reality, must serve as a wake-up call against educational complacency and low expectations.

In making this statement, Duncan advanced three empirically unsupportable claims about the meaningfulness of international test ranks often used by proponents of standardization: (1) the results from over sixty nations, and select Asian cities, on one international test of three subjects are comparable and meaningful indicators for policy making; (2) the rankings and results accurately describe the effectiveness of the U.S. public school system, the third largest system in the world, and the education systems in other countries and cities; and (3) the results explain cause-and-effect relationships between the economic strength of countries and cities who took the PISA and their education systems.

But wait! Despite all the impediments to the U.S. students ranking high as a group on PISA and other international tests, the results look very different when one compares apples to apples. However, one has to dig below the surface of the headlines to find those apples, and the truth. Unfortunately it looks like all the shovels are broken at the U.S. Department of Education (USDOE), but one is included in this book.

There exist inherent flaws in large standardized testing programs, and general impediments faced by PISA and other international tests of academic skills and knowledge that prevent them from attaining their lofty aims. The flaws make meaningful comparisons impossible. Those flaws include the (a) selective and disparate student testing populations within countries and cities; (b) influence of nonschool factors on testing outcomes; (c) curricular mismatches between tests and countries; and (d) the results do not correlate to other large-scale measures of innovation, creativity, entrepreneurship, or general economic strength of nations.

This chapter deconstructs the primitive and fraudulent claims made about the importance and usefulness of international test results and rankings as evidence of education quality and future economic security. It provides an evidence-based counternarrative to the "Kool-Aid" being served up by some politicians, OECD authors, education bureaucrats, and public school pundits to peddle standardization and homogenization of curriculum standards and student academic outputs.

Non-Comparable Results

As Gerald Bracey (2006) wrote, in order for two things to be compared, they must be comparable. Simply put, the structures and processes of international testing programs are not designed and implemented in ways that produce comparable results. But that does not stop authors of the assessments from making strong claims about what the results from their tests describe. For example, OECD authors of the PISA test stated the aims and claims of PISA prior to launching the first version in 2000:

> How well are young adults prepared to meet the challenges of the future? Are they able to analyse, reason, and communicate their ideas effectively? Do they have the capacity to continue learning throughout life? Parents, students, the public, and those who run education systems need to know. (OECD, 2000, p. 3)

There is no malicious or devious intent on the part of the developers and vendors of international tests. They are probably doing the best job they can analyzing the results and designing the best tests possible given the scale of the projects. However, the claims and comparisons made from the results do not stand up to serious scrutiny. One main impediment to the validity of international test results as accurate indicators of the quality of education and future economic strength of a nation or city is that the testing populations of many countries and cities simply do not compare well with those of the United States, or even among groups of nations.

The students in the testing samples of other countries are usually less poor than those in the United States. The testing samples represent only the students who remain in the school system by grade 8 or age 15, and generally the samples under-represent students with disabilities or second-language learners. In some cases, only select students from select cities within a country are included in the testing populations.

Much ink has been spilled by sinophiles, those enamored by the perceived brilliance of Chinese students, extolling the virtues of the education system in the People's Republic of China (China). Those accolades are based on the performance of a select group of students from Shanghai, who scored at the top of the 2012 PISA charts. In England, Phillips (2013) stated with exuberance that the children of China "will at least be part of an education system that appears to be paying great dividends."

Once again it seemed like the education sky was falling in the office of the former U.S. Secretary of Education Arne Duncan (2013) when he commented about the Shanghai results: "The big picture of U.S. performance on the 2012 PISA is straightforward and stark: It is a picture of educational stagnation. That brutal truth, that urgent reality, must serve as a wake-up call against educational complacency and low expectations."

In Germany, one headline summed up the general reaction of the press there to the Shanghai results, "Victory in PISA: China produces elite like a conveyor belt" (Grzanna, 2013). Authors of the PISA at the OECD wrote glowingly about Shanghai and stated, "The strength of their performance in mathematics, especially, is striking: In effect, the city's 15-year-olds scored the equivalent of nearly three years of schooling above students in most OECD countries" (Keeley, 2013). Similar praise can be found throughout the mainstream press from the 30 most industrialized countries that participated in the PISA 2012 testing.

Shanghai Surprise

One problem with praising the Shanghai results is that those doing the praising seem not to understand Bracey's (2006) rule about comparisons. Generally results from individual cities in China should not be included in analyses of international test results. When one digs below the surface, one finds the testing pool from Shanghai and the other Chinese cities included in PISA and other international tests do not represent the larger demographics of students in the Chinese education system. But the results do provide a good example of selective sampling from the PISA testing pool.

Zhao (2014) provided one of the most complete examples of how different the testing populations can be among cities and countries in his critique of Shanghai's 2012 PISA scores. Zhao explained in great detail that the testing population in Shanghai represents children from some of the richest families in the city. The students come predominately from homes with well-educated parents in professional careers and they attend the top performing high schools. Shanghai has more than 140,000 millionaires in a city with a total population of almost 23 million people.

The city has the third highest concentration of wealth in China, and the population is internationalized and much more highly educated than the general Chinese population. For example, almost 84 percent of the high school seniors in Shanghai go on to attend college (Shanghai.gov, 2013). That rate is more than three times the rate of high school students across China who are able to pursue college (Loveless, 2013). The wealth and family demographics of Shanghai are radically different than those of the country of China, where 29 percent of the total population, more than 392 million people (larger than the total U.S. population), live on $5 a day or less (World Bank, 2012).

But Shanghai is not the only city in the People's Republic of China that participates in international testing. Students from Hong Kong and Macao also score high on all subjects on every international test in which they participate. Like the samples from Shanghai, the testing populations of Hong Kong and Macao do not represent the country of China. Hong Kong and Macao are special administrative regions of the People's Republic of China, and their schools do not follow all of the standardization requirements of the Chinese system (Levin, 2012).

Over 90 percent of students in Hong Kong attend private schools, where there is much more autonomy over curriculum, teaching, and assessment. Those schools are much less standardized (OECD, 2013c, p. 56) and the students come from homes with highly educated and professional parents. Moreover, parents in Hong Kong, Shanghai, and Macao pay large sums of money to the principals of the top high schools to enroll their children, in effect creating super-schools for wealthy, high-achieving students. More of those selective super-schools take the international tests than average high schools, significantly skewing the testing samples in those cities (Levin, 2012).

In general, high school is not free in China. Although regulations now prohibit charging parents a fee for their children to attend high school, the practice continues, especially at the elite high schools. Only the students whose parents can afford to pay the "under the table" entrance fees are in the best schools at age 15 and only the ones that can pay handsomely are in quality schools. These realities limit the testing pool for the PISA tests in the People's Republic of China severely. Also, not all children are allowed to attend high school in the cities in which they live.

Some of the poorer children who live in Shanghai, Hong Kong, and other major cities in China are required to attend high school in their ancestral provinces (Loveless, 2013). Therefore, many students who might score lower on the PISA are not included in the PISA calculations for those cities because they cannot attend high school there. Also, there are not many students with special education needs in Shanghai, Hong Kong, or regular Chinese high schools. They are excluded from high-performing schools. Indeed, the enrollment rates for students with special needs in Chinese schools are lower than those in the United States, and many are not enrolled in school by age 15 when the PISA tests are given (Ringmar, 2013).

Paper Dragon

Yong Zhao (2015) pierces the veil of the education system in Peoples' Republic of China in his book *Who's Afraid of the Big Bad Dragon.* Zhao presents a historical analysis of the system and then deconstructs the current state of education in China to reveal that all that glitters might just be fake gold. The revelations about the weaknesses of the Chinese education system in the book are stunning. The Internet is also full of interesting revelations about the Chinese education system. Perhaps the USDOE does not know of Zhao's work or they did not pay their Wi-Fi bill for the past 10 years because bureaucrats there who praise China seem not to be aware of the limitations of the system.

The use of the Chinese education system to scare the American public into reforms that standardize and centralize public education is even more egregious when one considers that the majority of children in China never graduate high school. The opportunities to receive a quality education are limited in the cities and more reduced in the rural areas. According to Stanford University's Rural Education Action Program (REAP), only about 40 percent of children living in rural China attend high school, and only 35–45 percent of those students go on to graduate high school (REAP, 2013a). In addition, approximately 25 percent of middle school students drop out of school before entering high school (REAP, 2013b).

The percentage of middle school dropouts reaches about 60 percent in the rural areas (REAP, 2013b). The testing samples for "China" are so skewed that any results are meaningless. When the results for the entire country of "China" are reported for PISA and TIMSS, then it might be useful to include "China" in the testing samples for calculating ranks on international tests. PISA collects the data for other parts of China that participate in PISA but OECD officials are not allowed to report it. For now only the results for students in the richest, least standardized schools in some of the wealthiest cities in China are reported, yet their results masquerade as the overall nation of China.

Silly Sampling

The sampling issues exhibited by the testing populations from the People's Republic of China are replicated in other countries like Vietnam and other developing countries where large percentages of students are not in school at age 15 or even grade 8. Students who have special needs and second-language learners are also often excluded or not fully represented in testing samples. This is especially true in countries like Singapore, Korea, Japan, and the developing nations who participate in international testing.

The issues of sampling selectivity have been around since the inception of international testing. Simply put, the testing samples do not represent a comparison of apples to apples and the differences matter in terms of achievement on the tests. For example, student selectivity correlated positively with results on the SIMS in 1982 (Rotberg, 1990). The testing samples must be representative of all the students in a country and comparable to other countries for the results to have any usefulness.

The Second International Assessment of Educational Progress in Mathematics and Science (IAEPII) conducted in 1990–1991 included many examples of sample selectivity. For example, Russia tested only native speakers, Switzerland included only students in 15 of 26 cantons (states), Israel tested only students in Hebrew-speaking schools, and Spain restricted the sample population to Spanish-speaking schools and excluded students in Cataluna region (Lapointe, Mead, and Askew, 1992).

Likewise, the student samples used by many nations for the 1995 and 1999 TIMSS for grade 8 students would not meet the definition of random. Italy excluded entire provinces such as Sicily, its poorest province (Bracey, 1999). TIMSS officials included nonrepresentative cities like Hong Kong and Macao but they were advertised as representing "China." Conversely, the U.S. TIMSS samples for those years represented 98 percent of the available student population.

Once the international testing vendors solve the problem of sampling selectivity, then perhaps the ranks might become more meaningful. But as the next section explains, there are other serious factors that influence the usefulness of the rankings to guide education policy making and those factors make the results somewhat meaningless.

OUT OF SCHOOL FACTORS

Unfortunately, the United States has the highest level of childhood poverty in the industrialized world except for Romania and Bulgaria. The high poverty ranking affects its performance and rankings on international tests of academic achievement. There are multiple methods to calculate poverty, but regardless of the method, the results are similar: The United States has a high percentage of school-age children living in poverty. The OECD (2009) calculates childhood poverty using a harmonized international method.

According to the OECD (2009) researchers, "People are classified as poor when their equalized household income is less than half of the median prevailing in each country. . . . The poverty rate is a headcount of how many people fall below the poverty line" (p. 90). Approximately 23 percent of U.S. public school children lived in poverty in 2012 when one calculates poverty via the OECD harmonized definition of poverty.

The poverty threshold for a U.S. family of four during the 2011–2012 school year was $22,811 according to the National Center for Education Statistics (NCES), based on the official U.S. Census Bureau calculations. According to the NCES, more than 22 percent of U.S. public school children lived in poverty in 2012 when the PISA 2012 was administered compared to 15.6 percent in 2000.

The child poverty rate in a country explains up to 46 percent of the PISA scores in the 30 major industrialized countries in the world. Poverty has a similar influence on TIMSS results (OECD, 2013a, pp. 35–36). As a country's percentage of childhood poverty increases, its ranks on the PISA and TIMSS tests decrease (Mullis et al., 2012; OECD, 2013a). Poverty is an input variable. Proponents of standardization disregard poverty because inputs are not important in a performance-guarantee system.

The problem of childhood poverty is growing. In 2010, almost 48 percent of U.S. public school children qualified for either free or reduced priced school lunches. No other democratic OECD country boasts childhood poverty statistics like those. Consider that Finland and Denmark had less than 5 percent childhood poverty and Norway and Germany had less than 10 percent in 2010. Those countries continue to maintain childhood poverty below those rates today while the United States is struggling to keep its childhood poverty below 20 to 23 percent.

Furthermore, according to UNICEF (2013), the United States ranks 26th out of 29 industrialized countries in overall well-being of children, just ahead of Lithuania, Latvia, and Romania, but behind countries like Estonia, Hungary, and Slovakia; all countries that outranked the United States on PISA 2012 mathematics. The cumulative effects of poverty and its associated issues such as stress and frequent illness coalesce to depress overall academic achievement.

Regardless of which organization calculates the poverty rate, the United States ranks near the bottom of the industrialized world in terms of the percentage of its children living in poverty. During the period beginning with the administration of the 2011 TIMSS through the completion of the 2012 PISA testing, the U.S. child poverty rate ranged from 20 percent to 23 percent. Poverty exerts a negative influence on international tests scores and test scores in general in a variety of ways.

Standardized test results are heavily influenced by family human capital and community social capital (Sirin, 2005; Tienken and Mullen, 2014). Results from international tests are not immune to the influences of family and community. For example, the childhood poverty rate of a country can explain up to 46 percent of the test results on the TIMSS and PISA for the 30 most industrialized nations. The ranking of childhood poverty can accurately predict, within a few places, the rankings on PISA for the 30 most industrialized countries.

People who use worn out slogans about the importance for U.S. students to rank high on international tests need to wake up to the reality of what drives standardized test scores and start advocating to reduce childhood poverty in the United States as a solution to their fears of global competitiveness (e.g., Duncan, 2013; Hanushek and Wosseman, 2008). Reducing the childhood poverty level in the United States by half would propel international test rankings.

Models of Poverty

The PISA and TIMSS data tools make it easy to model the influence of various levels of poverty on U.S. scores and ranks (National Center for Education Statistics, n.d.). The aggregate U.S. scale score for the 2012 PISA mathematics section was 481. However, it is possible to model a less-poor America. U.S. public schools with 10 percent or less childhood poverty, about the same percentage of poverty as most of the 30 most industrialized countries that outrank the United States, scored 526. Another way to look it at is that U.S. schools with similar poverty levels as Finland outperform Finland on the PISA.

The scale score of 526 for less-poor U.S. schools is 45 points higher than the overall U.S. average that represents approximately 23 percent poverty. The 45-point difference moves the United States to 6th place for all countries that participated in the 2012 PISA math assessment, even when taking into account the selective sampling of some of those countries. Other countries with childhood poverty levels less than 10 percent that participated in PISA included, but are not limited to, Finland, Singapore, Netherlands, Switzerland, Japan, Korea, Austria, Australia, and the tested student population in Shanghai (OECD, 2014; Zhao, 2014).

Similar outcomes occur for the other tested subjects. For example, the average scale score for U.S. students on the 2012 PISA science test was 497, but the scale score for U.S. students in schools with 10 percent poverty or less was 546: a 49-point difference! That difference launches the United States from 23rd place to 2nd place among all other countries that took the test and not statistically significantly different ($p < 0.05$) than the first place rank of 551.

The same results occur in Reading. U.S. students in schools with 10 percent of the students or less living in poverty scored 554 compared to the impoverished U.S. average of 498. A difference of 56 scale score points is enough to put the United States 1st in the world compared to all other countries that took the test (NCES, n.d.; OECD, 2014). The vast differences in scores for less-poor students in the United States are not just a reality on the 2012 PISA. It extends to the latest version and earlier versions of the PISA as well. Poverty knows no time restraints.

The TIMSS Two-Step

Spoiler alert: U.S. public school students in eighth grade did not top the charts in TIMSS 2011 on either the mathematics or science sections, nor did they score at the top during any other administrations of the test. U.S. eighth-grade students ranked 7th out of the 40 countries that participated in the mathematics assessment. The average scale score for U.S. students was 509, compared with the international average of 500. But when one models TIMSS scores based on a vision of a less-poor American child, students in schools with 10 percent or less poverty had an average scale score of 537, putting them in 5th place, one point behind the selective testing population of the Russian Federation and 23 points ahead of students from Finland (NCES, n.d.).

Eighth-grade students achieved an average scale score of 525 on the science section. That secured 8th place. But less-poor students, those in schools with 10 percent or less poverty, achieved an average scale score of 558, and tied with Japan for 4th place. Reducing poverty from the current 20 to 23 percent to 10 percent eliminates almost the entire international test score "achievement lag" on PISA and TIMSS, in all sections, without standardizing or "reforming" anything with the education system. Reducing childhood poverty is a guaranteed way to raise total achievement in all subjects and increase global competitiveness.

Confidence in Mathematics

Childhood poverty affects learning in various ways and not always in ways that educators and parents might expect. Although childhood poverty, or the lack thereof, is most commonly associated with standardized test results, the question remains, how does poverty influence test results? Here is an interesting example unearthed in a PISA technical manual: mathematics self-efficacy. Self-efficacy can be related to confidence. For the sake of this example, let's just call it mathematics confidence or how well students think they can do math.

Some students believe they are good at math, while others do not. According to the 2012 PISA results, belief in one's ability to perform mathematics influences student achievement on the PISA math section. Analyses revealed that approximately 28 percent of the variance, or difference, on 2012 PISA mathematics test results was associated with student math confidence in the OECD countries, the most industrialized countries in the world (OECD, 2013b, pp. 83–86).

Self-efficacy has a 0.50 correlation to mathematics achievement on the PISA (OECD, 2013b, p. 83). A correlation that size suggests that there is a noticeable relationship between self-efficacy and math achievement. As self-efficacy rises, so too does mathematics PISA achievement in the industrialized countries. Countries where children had higher levels of self-efficacy also had higher PISA scores.

However, digging a little deeper, it's important to realize that poverty demonstrably relates to mathematical self-efficacy via anxiety. Math anxiety is related to math self-efficacy, and poorer students have more anxiety about math. Math anxiety accounted for an average of 14 percent of the variance in math scores (OECD, 2013b, p. 87), meaning that it dampens math achievement. More anxiety results in lower achievement. As already discussed, the United States has a high rate of child poverty. Consequently, the influence of anxiety and self-efficacy on PISA mathematics is stronger in the United States compared to other nations with lower child poverty.

The U.S. score difference between students with high and low self-efficacy levels was approximately 50-scale score points on the PISA 2012 math test (OECD, 2013b, p. 86). That difference would propel the U.S. students' score from 481 to 531, into 5th place on PISA mathematics, tied with Switzerland. The strong correlation between mathematical self-efficacy and mathematics achievement helps explain the strong relationship between poverty and mathematics achievement on the PISA because poverty influences self-efficacy.

So What?

The well-publicized international achievement lag of U.S. students seemingly disappears when one digs below the headline and compares nations based on the strongest predictor of student achievement, poverty. Even with the selective sampling of many other nations, U.S. public school students rank at the top or near the top of the world in reading, mathematics, and science when controlling for poverty.

However, the United States is not a nation of less-poor students, and as of 2015 over 50 percent of all public school students in the United States qualified for free or reduced lunch, an increase from the 2010 levels (Southern Education Foundation, 2015). Childhood poverty is increasing in the United States, not abating. According to PISA (OECD, 2013c, p. 29) researchers, only 10 percent of the variance in PISA results can be attributed to differences among international school systems whereas 36 percent is attributed to differences between schools and 54 percent is due to differences between students. Poverty creates differences between students and schools.

The average U.S. student lives in a low-income household and aggregate achievement of U.S. students on international tests is relatively low based on rankings on international tests. Standardizing curriculum expectations or outputs does not have a history of closing achievement gaps between rich and poor students. Standardizing curriculum expectations does not have a history of lifting children out of poverty. Standardization cements the existing social caste system.

Every country has achievement differences between rich and poor students as evidenced by international test results (OECD, 2013a, p. 72). The U.S. public school system does surprisingly well in terms of narrowing the achievement gap between rich and poor given the rhetoric to the contrary.

According to the OECD's data (2013a), the mathematics achievement variation between rich and poor students in the United States is "above average achievement and below average variation" (p. 55).

Students from poverty in the United States perform better than predicted on PISA math and the gap between rich and poor is smaller than expected. The so-called top performers like Shanghai, Japan, Singapore, Hong Kong, and Korea all have "above average performance and above average variation" (p. 55), indicating a larger gap between the performance of rich and poor students. The problem in the United States is that there exist so many students living in poverty compared to their peers in other industrialized nations that our aggregate scores look lower.

The lower ranking for U.S. students is Simpson's Paradox in action. Simpson's Paradox states that the results from an aggregate group, in this case the U.S. student population, are sometimes different than the results from the underlying subgroup data sets, like poor versus less-poor U.S. students. The U.S. sample is so populated with students from poverty, and poverty causes those students to score lower for a multitude of reasons, that the scores bring down the overall ranking for the country. Countries with less students in poverty are less affected by those students' lower results.

Standardization will not "fix" poverty or raise international test scores. As Tolstoy's (1887) enigmatic character from *Anna Karenina*, Levin, explained to his friend Sviazhsky, "What has to be cured is what makes him poor" (Tolstoy, Chapter 28). Education does not make one poor. It's not about increasing standardization to increase achievement; it's about decreasing poverty so children can take more advantage of the education resources they have.

Poverty aside, PISA results also point to the fact that less standardization might be needed to raise international tests rankings. The OECD (2013c, p. 52) reported a positive, moderate relationship of 0.32 between schools in OECD countries (the 30 most industrialized countries) that were less standardized and had greater autonomy over curriculum and assessment practices and overall achievement in mathematics. Compare that to one of the prized solutions of proponents of standardization: school competition.

According to OECD (2013c, p. 55), school competition has a 0.0004 relationship to math achievement on PISA. The United States actually underperforms in PISA math due in part to the extensive school competition in the United States. Meanwhile, U.S. public schools outperform private schools and charter schools on PISA math performance when testing samples are comparable but those are topics for another time (OECD, 2013c, pp. 55, 60).

One take away from the data presented thus far is that childhood poverty and autonomy over curriculum and assessment matter more in terms of student achievement than standardizing outputs across schools or countries.

But how much do low rankings on international tests really matter in terms of students' economic futures? According to the disciples of standardization, a lot, because the test ranks allegedly relate to national economic security and global competitiveness. What is the relationship between international test rankings and indicators of national economic strength?

Economic Hocus-Pocus

Several studies have been published since the inception of the NCLB era that challenged the notion that rankings on international tests predict or relate to national indicators of economic strength or productivity. But not all studies of international assessments are created equal. Some studies present positive relationships between ranks on tests like PISA and TIMSS and some show no relationship. The economic characteristics of the countries included in the samples of such studies are important because once again, in order to compare things, those things must be comparable.

If one is going to study relationships between education output and economic output, and make comparisons, then size matters. It does not make much practical, or global competitiveness-sense to compare countries with small populations and small economies, like Finland, Singapore, Switzerland, and Sweden, to some of the largest countries and economies on the planet, like that of the United States. Therefore, people who conduct studies about the relationships between international test ranks and economic strength should strive to use samples that include countries that are somewhat similar economically. They should use cluster sampling.

Correlations can be deceivingly positive, in favor of a relationship between international test ranks and economic strength of nations, when one includes all the countries from the TIMSS or PISA testing samples. That is because the smaller and poorer economies do tend to exhibit correlations between their test rankings and economic and industrial indicators (Tienken, 2008). For example, large improvements on the PISA or TIMSS rankings of a country like Tunisia could eventually, in the much longer term, lead to some economic growth because those improvements would most likely be linked to more students completing middle school and high school.

Because there are many more countries with smaller economies that administer the PISA and TIMSS tests than the G20 group of countries, the analysis samples can be artificially pollinated to produce statistically significant relationships because they are over-weighted with small and weak economies—Simpson's Paradox at work again. In actuality, simplistic conclusions, like the ones Hanushek and Woessmann (2008) provided, could be attributed to the fact that the results used to draw the conclusions were based on all countries in the PISA testing sample.

However, when one clusters the samples on the larger economies like the G20, the countries with the 19 largest economies on the planet, the results can be vastly different and fail to demonstrate meaningful relationships between rankings on PISA or TIMSS and large-scale economic indicators (Rameriz et al., 2006; Tienken, 2008). Results from earlier studies suggested that relationships between test rankings on international tests such as PISA and TIMSS and indicators of economic strength can be statistically significant and moderately strong when all the small economies like Serbia, Jordan, and Latvia remain in the sample with the G20 countries sample (Bracey, 2005; Hanushek and Woessmann, 2008; Rameriz et al., 2006).

Conversely, the relationship between international test ranks and indicators of economic strength can be negative, weak, or not statistically significant when only the participating G20 economies are in the sample (e.g., Bracey, 2007; Rameriz et al., 2006; Tienken, 2008). Once again, size matters, and cluster sampling is helpful when working with international comparisons. Beware of sweeping conclusions drawn from international test results from studies that did not use some form of cluster sampling.

Counterintuitive

In most cases there is no relationship between ranks on international tests and important economic indicators at the national level for the strongest economies in the world (Bracey, 2009; Tienken, 2008). In some cases the relationships between test ranks and economic indicators such a per capita cost of living adjusted income are actually negative for the strongest economies. The higher a country ranks on international tests the lower the per capita cost of living adjusted income (Baker, 2007; 2010) for the most industrialized countries.

Baker (2010) reported that the United States economically outcompetes every other nation that outranked it on the first international test ever administered, the First International Mathematics Study in 1964, the forerunner of the TIMSS:

> The United States produced more than $41,000 a year for every family of four than did the nations scoring higher in 1964. Topping it off, the correlation between test scores and economic success across nations was negative on six of the measures, reaching a whopping r = –0.58 for Qualify of Life and r = –0.48 for rate of economic growth. (p. 62)

Interestingly, the countries that outranked the United States on the every international test administered have not and will not eclipse the United States economically based on education output.

The United States economically out-produces every country that outranked it on every international test since 1964, on every major economic measure. In other cases the relationship between test rankings and economic growth is counterintuitive. Bils and Klenow (1998) demonstrated that the relationship between international test rankings and national economic growth might actually move in opposite directions; better test rankings might be driven by better economics in the G20, not by better education systems.

Harbison and Myers (1956) raised the specter of the counterintuitive relationship almost a decade before the administration of the first international test when they wrote, "Education is both the seed and flower of economic development" (p. xi). A strong economy might be an important factor in better test results on international tests for the largest economies because stronger economies generally translate into better living conditions for children, generally.

Tienken and Tramaglini (2017) tested the counterintuitive ideas and findings put forth by Bils and Klenow (1998) as well as Harbison and Myers (1956), and found that for the G20 countries, education does in fact need the economy. They used a basket of indicators to create a proxy for overall economic strength from 1994 to 2005 and ran correlations to the rankings on the TIMSS and PISA international tests of math and science administered during that period.

The results suggested strong, statistically and practically significant relationships between the economic strength of G20 economies in the decade leading up to the administration of an international test and the country's ranking. The authors identified strong, positive correlation coefficients ranging from 0.705 to 0.856. Economic conditions influence student achievement in the G20 countries yet proponents of standardization, and PISA and TIMSS authors say the tail wags the economic dog.

All Hat, No Cattle

The idiom *All Hat, No Cattle* is an appropriate way to categorize results from international tests. The phrase originates from the American West to describe people who look the part of a rancher but have no experience. They parade around in their rancher costumes and meanwhile they do not know how to ride a horse. *All Hat, No Cattle* is a general derogatory phrase to describe someone who pretends to be something he is not.

Authors of TIMSS and PISA claim that the results provide important information about how prepared students are for future success in a knowledge economy. The PISA and TIMSS authors draw inferences and make strong claims about a country's overall competitiveness and future economic security based on the percentage of students in each participating country who achieve at the highest of the six PISA achievement levels.

For instance, authors from the OECD (2013a) claimed that the PISA achievement levels correlated to the preparedness of a nation's cohort of 15-year-old students to compete economically in the global economy.

> Performance in PISA refers to particular and increasingly complex tasks students are able to complete. A small proportion of students attains the highest levels and can be called top performers in mathematics, reading, or science. Even fewer are the academic all-rounders, those students who achieve proficiency Level 5 or higher in mathematics, reading, and science simultaneously. These students will be at the forefront of a competitive, knowledge-based global economy. They are able to draw on and use information from multiple and indirect sources to solve complex problems. (p. 64)

The PISA authors make a stunning claim that the results from the PISA have a cause-and-effect relationship to future economic success for students. The claim is stunning, first because the test was not designed to provide that kind of information. There is nothing in the construction of the test that provides for measuring the influence of the PISA rankings on economic growth or strength.

Secondly, it is a leap of empirical faith that the results from one measurement of knowledge and skills of a 15-year-old, from one test of a narrow set of knowledge and skills, at one point in time, will remain static for the remainder of the teenager's life, including adulthood when they actually begin to contribute to the economy. It is as if the PISA authors believe the teenager will cease all learning and academic growth from age 15 onward. The PISA statement is also stunning in its demonstration of the simplistic, linear thinking about how knowledge is obtained, applied, nurtured, and translated into economic output.

Not to be outdone by PISA authors, the former U.S. Secretary of Education under President Barack Obama, Arne Duncan (2012), made similar statements about the importance of ranking high on international tests in order to secure a vibrant economic future in his comments about the TIMSS 2011 results:

> Given the vital role that science, technology, engineering, and math play in stimulating innovation and economic growth, it is particularly troubling that eighth-grade science achievement is stagnant and that students in Singapore and Korea are far more likely to perform at advanced levels in science than U.S. students. A number of nations are out-educating us today in the STEM disciplines—and if we as a nation don't turn that around, those nations will soon be out-competing us in a knowledge-based, global economy. (p. 1)

Similar to the primitive comments made by the PISA authors, Duncan transformed the levels of achievement on the TIMSS eighth-grade math and science tests into indicators of overall global competitiveness of U.S. students, and the country as a whole in the areas of science, technology, and mathematics, although technology is not tested on international tests. Duncan's characterization of the TIMSS results was like a statistical magic show deserving of top billing in Las Vegas.

Duncan forwarded the false premise that students from countries that outranked U.S. students will somehow work to eclipse the economic dominance of the United States and take high-quality jobs, and the economic future from U.S. students in the future. Although the rhetoric used by vendors of international testing sounds powerful and authoritative, it is really just dogma and worn out slogans left over from the Sputnik era, mixed with a little snake oil (Tienken and Orlich, 2013). The rhetoric and claims lack substance and empirical evidence. They are all hat, no cattle.

Globally Competitive

Proponents of education standardization consistently forward a narrative about the global competitiveness of the United States. The global economy has been referred to as the "knowledge economy" (Duncan, 2013), innovation economy (Massachusetts Institute of Technology [MIT], 2013), conceptual economy (U.S. Council on Competitiveness [USCOC], 2007), and the creative economy (Howkins, 2001; Martin Prosperity Institute, 2015). Regardless of what commentators on global competitiveness call it, the terms *knowledge, innovation, conceptual, and creative* signify that a focus on competencies such as knowledge regurgitation, process imitation, and literal comprehension are no longer enough to produce citizens intellectually equipped to grow the 19 largest economies on the planet.

The previous economic focus on nineteenth-century skills for the industrial revolution has shifted to competencies associated with creativity, innovation, and entrepreneurship (Wagner, 2008; World Economic Forum, 2013). It is now a focus on diversity of talents, not the homogenization of talent that is necessary for an uncertain future. The U.S. economy is vastly more diversified than it was at the turn of the nineteenth century and a wider range of skills and dispositions are necessary.

The results from the 2012 Global Chief Executive Officer Study conducted by the IBM Corporation made several recommendations for the skills necessary in the global economy. The recommendations run counter to the skills assessed on the PISA and TIMSS tests and call into question the use of PISA and TIMSS results as indicators of an individual being prepared for the global economy. According to 1,700 CEOs representing 64 countries and 18 major industries, leaders and employees in the global economy must be able to (a) innovate, (b) collaborate and cooperate (globally among themselves and with their customer bases), (c) be creative, (d) seek opportunity, (e) use complexity to a strategic advantage, and (f) be communicative (pp. 21–24).

The USCOC (2012) cited innovation, entrepreneurship, flexibility, and creativity as key factors necessary to drive the U.S. knowledge economy in the future. Relative to its earlier Competitiveness Index, the USCOC (2007) cited the United States as the global role model of an entrepreneurial economy. Zhao (2012) warned that American policy makers are making the wrong bet by using results from international tests to drive standardization policies that mandate curricula and assessments that place a premium on the development and demonstration of routine academic skills. The routine academic skills valued in a standardized education environment are the same ones easily offshored to countries that pay substantially lower wages.

Reimers (2009) cited many of the skills and dispositions recommended in the IBM study (IBM Corp., 2012) as important for people to possess in the future in order to cope with the fast changing nature of work and society in general. George (2012) identified risk-taking, creativity, innovation, and entrepreneurship as critical skills for business leaders and employees in order for the United States to increase its global competitiveness. The World Competitiveness Center (2013) echoed the need for innovative and entrepreneurial skills for the United States to maintain its consistently high rankings on the World Competitiveness Index.

The World Economic Forum (WEF) (Gray, 2016) identified (a) complex problem solving, (b) critical thinking, creativity, (c) people management, (d) coordinating with others, (e) emotional intelligence, (f) judgment and decision-making, (g) service orientation, (h) negotiation, (i) cognitive flexibility, (j) active listening, and (k) quality control as the skills and dispositions that will drive what WEF calls the fourth industrial revolution within the next 10 years. The WEF researchers predict that creativity will be the most important skill for future global competitiveness because it is difficult to outsource.

Not-So Basic Skills

One might assume, given the bureaucratic rhetoric by leaders such as the U.S. secretaries of education and claims by the researchers of PISA and TIMSS that the results from PISA and TIMSS relate strongly to skills and dispositions required in the knowledge economy. Creativity, innovation, and entrepreneurship are examples of unstandardized skills and dispositions that are valued in the knowledge economy and identified as important by leaders in various fields.

The basic skills measured by international tests are not the competencies that will propel a large, developed economy forward (Auerswald, 2012; Zhao, 2012). Krueger and Lindhal (2001) found that countries with high levels of education attainment see no effect on national economic growth by incremental increases in the populations' levels of classical education. Their findings suggest that the knowledge economy does not grow via the application of nineteenth-century skills of computation and comprehension that tests like PISA and TIMSS measure. Perhaps the engine of economic growth for a large economy like that of the United States relies more on the execution of competencies harder to measure.

Skills and Dispositions for 2060

Most of the crop of preschool students from 2017 will enter the full-time workforce between the years 2035 and 2040. Job market predictions by the U.S. Bureau of Labor Statistics (USBLS, 2012) forecast to around 2025 as of 2016, so it is difficult to project what the employment landscape might look like beyond that timeframe. However, given the growing trend by U.S. multinational corporations of offshoring jobs that require routine skills to the countries with the lowest wages and least protective worker and environmental regulations, one could conjecture that skills and dispositions that are difficult to offshore—creativity, innovation, and entrepreneurship—will retain value in 2035 and beyond.

For the purposes of this book skills are defined as things students can do, like cooperate, communicate, and problem solve. Dispositions are defined as purposefully developed habits or ways one acts that are learned such as empathy, compassion, and courage. Importantly, skills and dispositions like creativity, cooperation, courage, compassion, innovation, strategizing, networking, and entrepreneurship are uniquely unstandardized.

Such skills and dispositions will be valuable to the 2017 cohort of preschool students not only in 2036 when they need to live independent and humanely productive lives in a democracy, but also in 2050 and 2060 when they need to remain economically viable in their chosen professions. Skills and dispositions necessary for an uncertain future transcend time and cannot be standardized. They are best developed in an unstandardized education environment.

International Math Does Not Add Up

The TIMSS and PISA ranks do not equate to rankings on international measures of creativity, innovation, and entrepreneurship. In fact, TIMSS and PISA tests measure skills related to the late nineteenth and early twentieth centuries. Sjoberg (2012) demonstrated that many of the PISA questions lack authentic context and they do not require creative or innovative thinking, the type of thinking that drives a knowledge economy.

Also, Sjoberg documented that students from different countries take different parts of the PISA test, a fact that destroys the claim that every student completes the exact same exam. In addition, he demonstrated how the translation process also aids students from some languages more than others by accidently providing context clues that give away the correct answer (Sjoberg, 2012). Sjoberg has been an outspoken, research-based critic of PISA and TIMSS and documented multiple issues with the tests that render the results impotent for policy making (Sjoberg, 2016; 2012).

Stewart (2013) provided a blistering critique of the PISA and stated that the questions do not measure innovative skills, the results were flawed, and that the statistics used to arrive at the results are "utterly wrong" (p. 2). Dancis (2014) illustrated how the majority of the so-called most challenging PISA mathematics questions required students to solve only multistep arithmetic word problems: not algebra or geometry. The mathematical thinking required on the PISA is not complex. It is convergent and routine.

Likewise, Martio's (2009) work further supports an assertion made in this chapter that much of the mathematics content on the PISA test is derived from early twentieth-century thinking. Martio concluded that the PISA math test falls short of reflecting the type or level of innovative math necessary to compete in a global economy. The TIMSS math tests for grades 4 and 8 suffer the same limitations that most other large-scale standardized have: They can't deliver the goods in terms of measuring accurately the skills needed in the innovation economy.

Rutkowski, Rukowski, and Plucker (2015) cautioned that the PISA results cannot provide usable information about teaching and learning due to the design of the test. They also warned that the content of the tests comes from what one international organization, the OECD, deems as important. The authors conclude that PISA might not capture important learning and cultural outcomes of U.S. students as they pertain to global competitiveness.

Tienken and Mullen (2014) conducted a study that explained the relationships between mathematics rankings from TIMSS 1995 and 1999 and PISA 2000 and 2003 and international indices of creativity, innovation, and entrepreneurship within the G20 countries. They used the (a) Global Entrepreneurship and Development Index (Acs and Szerb, 2010), (b) Global Creativity Index (Martin Prosperity Institute, 2011), and (c) Global Innovation Index (Dutta and Lanvin, 2013). They set the level of statistical significance at the generally acceptable level in social science of $p \leq 0.05$ (Krathwohl, 2009).

Tienken and Mullen found no statistically or practically significant relationships between the age cohorts who took those international tests and results from indices later in life that measured the skills and dispositions necessary in the innovation economy. That is most likely because international tests of student academic knowledge and skills cannot measure skills and dispositions that are difficult to standardize, like creativity, innovation, and entrepreneurship.

Rules for Testing

Apart from not being able to justify with evidence the claims they make about the importance of the results from tests like TIMSS and PISA, authors of international tests and those who peddle inaccurate conclusions about their results have another problem: validity of results. The seventh edition of the *Standards for Educational and Psychological Testing*, developed by a joint committee represented by members of the American Educational Research Association (AERA), American Psychological Association (APA), and National Council on Measurement in Education (NCME), provides straightforward, research-based guidance on test development and use. The Standards are separated into 12 categories and provide specific recommendations on topics that include validity of results and interpretations, test design and development, and responsible use of standardized tests and results (AERA et al., 2014). The standards also describe the rights and responsibilities of test takers.

Standard 1.0 provides general guidance regarding validity of results for uses related to various types of standardized testing contexts such as employment, education program placement, college entrance, and diagnostics. The Standard states, "Clear articulation of each intended test score interpretation for a specified use should be set forth, and appropriate validity evidence in support of each intended interpretation should be provided" (AERA et al., 2014, p. 23). Standard 1.1 expands on this guidance: "No test permits interpretations that are valid for all purposes or in all situations. Each recommended interpretation for a given use requires validation" (AERA et al., 2014, p. 23).

Standard 1.1 recommends "a rationale should be presented for each intended interpretation of test scores for a given use, together with a summary of the evidence and theory bearing on the intended interpretation" (AERA et al., 2014, p. 23). Based on general guidance from Standard 1.0 and Standard 1.1, authors of international tests should provide transparent evidence of validity for each interpretation or claim they make. The guidance also implies that using results from one test for multiple interpretation purposes might not be valid. It is incumbent upon those who use the results from one test in multiple ways to present appropriate evidence that demonstrates the results from the test can be used in those ways.

For example, there needs to be evidence to validate the results from the TIMSS and PISA tests as (a) predictors of future economic strength of nations, (b) career readiness of students, (c) quality of a nation's education system, and (d) preparedness of students for postsecondary education experiences, to just name a few. Based on the existing evidence, PISA and TIMSS results flunk the validity tests for the aforementioned uses for the G20 countries and for the 20 strongest economies on planet as ranked by the World Economic Forum's Global Competitiveness Index (Baker, 2010; Sjoberg, 2016; 2012; Tienken, 2008; Tienken and Mullen, 2014).

It is curious to note that the results from TIMSS and PISA tests also do not relate well to the career readiness of students or postsecondary participation in the G20. The countries ranking in the top 10 for math and science do not go on to produce the highest quality scientists, as will be explained in chapter 3. Nor do the highest-ranking countries produce the highest percentage of people who achieve masters and doctorate degrees. The results from international tests just do not hold up well to established standards for validity and interpretation.

Ignorance or Opinion

Proponents of standardization who use the rankings of U.S. students on international tests are either misinformed or are knowingly misinforming the public about the importance of those rankings to justify their policy preferences. Neither explanation is acceptable when making education policy for over 56 million children who attend public school. Everyone is entitled to his or her own opinion, but opinions should not drive policy making when facts are readily available. The results from international tests cannot be used to justify policies that seek to standardize and homogenize the U.S. public school system with inert sets of generic performance-guarantee statements.

Socrates articulated the difference between fact and opinion by explaining that opinion resides somewhere between *what is* (knowledge) and *what is not* (ignorance). He stated, "Many conventional views held by most people . . . hover somewhere between what is not and what fully is" (Plato, *Republic*. 203d. Translated by Kamtekar, 2003). Socrates described that those who have the "eyes" to seek the facts but are unable (or unwilling), even with the help of a guide, give opinions. However, it "cannot be said that they know any of the things they hold opinions about" (Plato, *Republic*. Translated by Kamtekar, 2003). Opinions are not facts.

One explanation for the continued misuse of results from international tests to drive standardization policies might be, as Socrates stated, that those people with the power to influence, create, and/or manage education policies have the ability to understand and correctly interpret results from international tests but choose not to do so. Therefore, their utterances about the importance of the results should be regarded as nothing more than opinions about a topic which they choose not to know.

Next Steps

The United States has remained one of the most creative, innovative, and economically dominant nations on the planet since the end of World War II. Claims of imminent economic and national security demise at the hands of what were advertised as educationally superior nations have not materialized in more than 60 years. Whether it be the Soviets after the launch of *Sputnik 1*, the Japanese domination of the steel and auto industries during the 1980s, the ascendancy of India in the software and remote call center markets in the late 1990s, or the rise of China as a world power, the rhetoric is always the same. The lagging achievement by U.S. students on international tests is the cause for concern and the United States is losing its global competitiveness to what are purported to be educationally advanced nations (Maiello, 2014; Tienken and Orlich, 2013). Hence, there is a need to standardize.

But you can't standardize creativity, innovation, or entrepreneurship. The next chapter presents an argument that the United States is one of the most creative and innovatively advanced nations on the planet and has been for a long time. The fruits of education sometimes take a long time to ripen. Chapter 3 contains data from longer-term indicators of education output and argues, with evidence, that a less standardized system might be superior to the one in which the preschool classes of 2017 and beyond inherited from misguided and ideological policy making.

REFERENCES

Acs, Z.J. & Szerb, L. (2010, June). *The global entrepreneurship and development index (GEDI).* Paper presented at the DRUID summer conference, London. Retrieved from http://www2.druid.dk/conferences/viewpaper.php?id=502261&cf=43.

American Education Research Association (AERA), American Psychological Association (APA), & National Council on Measurement in Education (NCME). (2014). *Standards for educational and psychological testing.* Washington, DC: American Education Research Association.

Auerswald, P. (2012). *The coming prosperity: How entrepreneurs are transforming the global economy.* New York: Oxford University Press.

Baker, K. (2010). A bad idea: National standards based on test scores. *AASA Journal of Scholarship and Practice, 7*(3), 60–67.

Baker, K. (2007). Are international test scores worth anything? *The Phi Delta Kappan, 89*(2), 101–104.

Bils, M. & Klenow, P.J. (1998). *Does schooling cause growth, or the other way around?* (Working paper No. 6393).

Bracey, G.W. (2009, January 9). International comparisons. More fizzle than fiz. *Huffington Post.* Retrieved from http://www.huffingtonpost.com/gerald-bracey/international-comparisons_b_149690.html.

Bracey, G.W. (2007). Test scores and economic growth. *Phi Delta Kappan, 88*(7), 554–556.

Bracey, G.W. (2006). *Reading educational research: How to avoid getting statistically snookered.* Portsmouth, NH: Heinneman.

Bracey, G.W. (2005). Research: Put out over PISA. *Phi Delta Kappan, 86*(10), 797–798.

Bracey, G. (1999). The propaganda of "A Nation at Risk." Retrieved from http://www.america-tomorrow.com/bracey/EDDRA/EDDRA8.htm.

Dancis, J. (2014). What does the international PISA math test really tell us? *AASA Journal of Scholarship and Practice*, 10(4), 31-34. Retrieved from http://www.aasa.org/jsp.aspx.

Duncan, A. (2013, December 3). *The threat of educational stagnation and complacency.* Retrieved from http://www.ed.gov/news/speeches/threat-educational-stagnation-and-complacency.

Duncan, A. (2012, December 11). *Statement by U.S. Secretary of Education Arne Duncan on the release of the 2011 TIMSS and PIRLS assessments*. Retrieved from http://www.ed.gov/news/press-releases/statement-us-secretary-education-arne-duncan-release-2011-timss-and-pirls-assess.

Dutta, S. & Lanvin, B. (Eds.). (2013). *Global innovation index 2013: The local dynamics of innovation* (6th ed.). Geneva, Switzerland: Cornell University, INSEAD, and World Intellectual Property Organization.

George, B. (2012, March 12). Developing global leaders is America's competitive advantage. *Harvard Business Review Blog Network.* Retrieved from http://blogs.hbr.org/2012/03/developing-global-leaders-is-a/.

Gray, A. (2016, January 19). The 10 skills you will need to thrive in the fourth industrial revolution. *World Economic Forum.* Retrieved from http://www.weforum.org/agenda/2016/01/the-10-skills-you-need-to-thrive-in-the-fourth-industrial-revolution.

Grzanna, M. (2013, December 3). Victory in Pisa: China produces elite like a conveyor belt. *N-tv.* Retrieved from http://www.n-tv.de/politik/China-produziert-Elite-wie-am-Fliessband-article11848981.html.

Hanushek, E.A. & Woessmann, L. (2008). The role of cognitive skills in economic development. *Journal of Economic Literature, 46*(3), 607–668.

Harbison, F. & Myers, C. (Eds.). (1956). *Manpower and education.* New York: McGraw-Hill.

Howkins, J. (2001). *The creative economy: How people make money from ideas.* London: Penguin.

IBM Corp. (2012). *Leading through connections: Insights from the global chief executive officer study*. CEO C-Suite Studies.

Kamtekar, R. (2003). *Plato: The Republic*. London: Penguin Books.

Keeley, B. (2013, December 3). Asia's students storm PISA 2012. *OECD Insights.* Retrieved from http://oecdinsights.org/2013/12/03/asias-students-storm-pisa-2012/.

Krathwohl, D.R. (2009). *Methods of educational & social science research: An integrated approach* (3rd ed.). Long Grove, IL: Waveland Press.

Krueger, A.B., & Lindhal, M. (2001, December). Education for growth: Why and for whom? *Journal of Economic Literature, 39*, 1101–1136.

Lapointe, A.E., Askew, J.M., & Mead, N.A. (1992) *Learning science*. Princeton, NJ: Educational Testing Service.

Levin, D. (2012, November 12). A Chinese education, for a price. *New York Times*. Retrieved from http://www.nytimes.com/2012/11/22/world/asia/in-china-schools-a-culture-of-bribery-spreads.html?_r=0.

Loveless, T. (2013). *PISA's China problem.* Brookings. Retrieved from http://www.brookings.edu/blogs/brown-center-chalkboard/posts/2013/10/09-pisa-chinaproblem-loveless.

Maiello, M. (2014, January 13). The Japanese just bought Jim Beam. Remember when they owned the Empire State Building? *Esquire*. Retrieved from http://www.esquire.com/food-drink/drinks/news/a26838/japanWese-bought-jim-beam/.

Martin Prosperity Institute. (2015). *The global creativity index 2015*. Toronto, ON: MPI. Retrieved from http://martinprosperity.org/media/Global-Creativity-Index-2015.pdf.

Martin Prosperity Institute. (2011). *Creativity and prosperity: The 2010 global creativity index*. Toronto, ON: MPI. Retrieved from http://martinprosperity.org/2011/10/01/creativity-and-prosperity-the-global-creativity-index/.

Martio, O. (2009). Long-term effects of learning mathematics in Finland: Curriculum changes and calculators. *Teaching of Mathematics, 12*(2), 51–56.

Massachusetts Institute of Technology. (MIT). (2013). *Report of the MIT Task Force on Innovation and Production.* Author. Retrieved from http://web.mit.edu/press/images/documents/pie-report.pdf.

Mullis, I.V.S., Martin, M.O., Foy, P., & Arora, A. (2012). *TIMSS 2011 international results in mathematics*. Chestnut Hill, MA: Boston College.

National Center for Education Statistics [NCES]. (n.d.). *International data explorer*. Author. Retrieved from http://nces.ed.gov/surveys/international/ide/.

Organisation for Economic Co-operation and Development [OECD]. (2014). *PISA 2012 results in focus*. Author, OECD Publishing. Retrieved from http://www.oecd.org/pisa/keyfindings/pisa-2012-results-overview.pdf.

Organisation for Economic Co-operation and Development [OECD]. (2013a). *PISA 2012 results: What students know and can do: Student performance in reading, mathematics and science*. Vol. I. PISA, OECD Publishing. Retrieved from http://www.oecd.org/pisa/keyfindings/pisa-2012-results-volume-I.pdf.

Organisation for Economic Co-operation and Development [OECD]. (2013b). *PISA 2012 results: Ready to learn. Students' engagement, drive, and self-beliefs.* Vol. III. Author, OECD Publishing. Retrieved from http://www.oecd.org/pisa/keyfindings/PISA-2012-results-volume-III.pdf.

Organisation for Economic Co-operation and Development [OECD]. (2013c). *PISA 2012 results: What makes schools successful? Resources, policies and practices.* Vol. IV. PISA , OECD Publishing. Retrieved from http://www.oecd.org/pisa/keyfindings/pisa-2012-results-volume-IV.pdf.

Organisation for Economic Co-operation and Development [OECD]. (2009). *Society at a glance*. Author, OECD Publishing. p. 90. Retrieved from http://www.oecd-ilibrary.org/social-issues-migration-health/society-at-a-glance-2009_soc_glance-2008-en.

Organisation for Economic Co-operation and Development [OECD]. (2000). *Measuring student skills and knowledge: The PISA 2000 assessment of reading, mathematical, and scientific literacy*. Author, OECD Publishing. Retrieved from http://www.oecd.org/education/school/programmeforinternationalstudentassessmentpisa/33692793.pdf.

Phillips, T. (2013, December 4). PISA education tests: Why Shanghai pupils are so special. *The Telegraph*. Retrieved from http://www.telegraph.co.uk/news/worldnews/asia/china/10494678/PISA-education-tests-Why-Shanghai-pupils-are-so-special.html.

Rameriz, F.O., Luo, X., Schofer, E., & Meyer, J.W. (2006). Student achievement and national economic growth. *American Journal of Education, 113*, 1–29.

Reimers, F.M. (2009). Leading for global competency. *Educational Leadership, 67*(1). Retrieved from http://www.ascd.org/publications/educational-leadership/sept09/vol67/num01/Leading-for-Global-Competency.aspx.

Ringmar, S. (2013, December 28). Here's the truth about Shanghai schools: They're terrible. *The Guardian*. Retrieved from http://www.theguardian.com/commentisfree/2013/dec/28/shanghai-china-schools-terrible-not-ideal.

Rural Education Action Program. (2013a). Keeping kids in school. *Stanford University*. Retrieved from http://reap.stanford.edu/docs/research_projects__keeping_kids_in_school.

Rural Education Action Program. (2013b). Money for matriculation: REAP Brief #114. *Stanford University*. Retrieved from http://iis-db.stanford.edu/pubs/23435/REAP114-EN.pdf.

Rutkowski, D., Rutkowski, L., & Plucker, J.A. (2015). Should individual U.S. school participate in PISA? *Phi Delta Kappan, 96*(4), 68–73.

Rotberg, I.C. (1990, December). I never promised you first place. *Phi Delta Kappan*, pp. 296–303.

Shanghai.gov. (2013). *Regular Education*. Author. Retrieved from http://www.shanghai.gov.cn/shanghai/node17256/node17432/node17446/ userobject22ai22041.html.

Sirin, S.R. (2005). Socioeconomic status and academic achievement: A meta-analytic review of research. *Review of Educational Research, 75*(3), 417–453.

Sjoberg, S. (2016). OECD, PISA, and globalization. The influence of the international assessment regime. In C. Tienken & C. Mullen (Eds.), *Education policy perils: Tackling the tough issues* (pp. 102–133). Philadelphia, PA: Taylor Francis Routledge.

Sjoberg, S. (2012). PISA: Politics, fundamental problems and intriguing results [English trans.]. *La Revue, Recherches en Education, 14*, 1–21. Retrieved from http://www.scienceinpublic.com.au/blog/wp-content/uploads/Svein-Sjoberg-PISA-tests_La-Revue_no14-Sept-2012.pdf.

Southern Education Foundation. (2015). *A new majority research bulletin: Low income students now a majority in nation's public schools*. Author. Retrieved from http://www.southerneducation.org/Our-Strategies/Research-and-Publications/New-Majority-Diverse-Majority-Report-Series/A-New-Majority-2015-Update-Low-Income-Students-Now.

Stewart, W. (2013, July 31). Is PISA fundamentally flawed? *TES magazine*. Retrieved from http://www.tes.co.uk/article.aspx?storycode=6344672.

Tienken, C.H. & Tramaglini, T.W. (2017, in press). International test rankings and student academic performance: It's the economy stupid. In D. Sharpes (Ed.),

Handbook on comparative and international education. New York: Information Age Press.

Tienken, C.H. & Mullen, C.A. (2014). The curious case of international student assessment: Rankings and realities in the innovation economy. In S. Harris & J. Mixon (Eds.), *Building cultural community through global educational leadership* (pp.146–164). Ypsilanti, MI: NCPEA Press.

Tienken, C.H. & Orlich, D.C. (2013). *The school reform landscape: Fraud, myth, and lies*. New York: Rowman and Littlefield.

Tienken, C.H. (2008). Rankings of international achievement test performance and economic strength: Correlation or conjecture. *International Journal of Education Policy and Leadership, 3*(4), 1–15.

Tolstoy, L. (1887/2002). *Anna Karenina*. New York: Signet.

Tramaglini, T.W. & Tienken, C.H. (2016). Customized curriculum and high achievement in high poverty schools. In C. Tienken & C. Mullen (Eds.). *Education policy perils: Tackling the tough issues* (pp. 75–101). Philadelphia, PA: Taylor Francis.

UNICEF Office of Research. (2013). *Child well-being in rich countries: A comparative overview*. Innocenti Report Card 11, UNICEF Office of Research, Florence. Retrieved from http://www.unicef-irc.org/publications/pdf/rc11_eng.pdf.

U.S. Bureau of Labor Statistics (USBLS). (2012). *Employment projects 2022*. Retrieved from http://www.bls.gov/emp/ep_table_103.htm.

U.S. Council on Competitiveness (USCOC). (2012). *Clarion call. A look back and a path forward*. Author. Retrieved from http://www.compete.org/images/uploads/File/PDF%20Files/CoC_2013_Clarion_FINAL.pdf.

U.S. Council on Competitiveness (USCOC). (2007). *Competitiveness index: Where America Stands*. Author. Retrieved from http://www.compete.org/publications/detail/357/competitiveness-index-where-america-stands/.

Wagner, Tony. (2008). *The global achievement gap: Why even our best schools don't teach the new survival skills our children need—and what we can do about it*. New York: Basic Books.

World Bank. (2012). *Poverty headcount ratio at $2 a day (PPP)*. Author. Retrieved from http://data.worldbank.org/indicator/SI.POV.2DAY.

World Competitiveness Center. (2013). *World competitiveness ranking*. Lausanne, Switzerland: Institute for Management Development.

World Economic Forum. (2013). *The global competitiveness report: 2013–2014*. Geneva: Author.

Zhao, Y. (2015). *Who's afraid of the big bad dragon? Why China has the best (and worst) education system in the world*. Hoboken, NJ: Wiley.

Zhao, Y. (2014, March 29). *How does PISA put the world at risk (Part 4): Misleading the world*. Retrieved from http://zhaolearning.com/2014/03/29/how-does-pisa-put-the-world-at-risk-part-4-misleading-the-world/.

Zhao, Y. (2012). *World class learners: Educating creative and entrepreneurial students*. New York: Corwin Press.

Chapter 3

Global Dominance

The argument vended to the American public for the need to standardize curriculum expectations and student academic output, based on claims that the United States is losing its global competitiveness because of lagging achievement of U.S. students on international tests, is fatally flawed. The advertised importance of the achievement lag of U.S. students on international tests, and the corresponding solution of standardization, do not stand up to scrutiny, although they make for great headlines in the press. The United States is one of the most economically competitive countries on the planet and it is not losing its competitive advantage due to perceived public education failings.

Educating the approximately 56 million students that attend public school each year is a long-term process. The fruits of education labor might not present themselves immediately or in ways that can be measured efficiently. Some of the hard work a kindergarten teacher accomplishes day-in and day-out with his or her class might not result in visible or measurable results until the following year, or even later. The socially conscious, problem-based approach used by the middle school teaching team to help connect new content to students' experiences might not yield easily measurable outcomes, especially in April or May, when most state education bureaucrats like to mandate standardized testing.

I submit that the education output that proponents of standardization claim the United States lacks, the output they say will secure a globally competitive future for the U.S. economy, must be measured in the longer term, not the short term, and certainly not by the means that standardizing proponents use to monitor the implementation of one-size-fits-all programs. The outputs of the system of public education must be viewed through long-term, diverse indicators of global economic competitiveness. In this chapter, I present some indicators that provide a long view of education output.

Globally Competitive

Fast-forward from the claim by Harbison and Myers (1956) that economics drives education in the world's largest economies to the release of the Massachusetts Institute of Technology (MIT, 2013) report on innovation and production. The results of the MIT study presented in the report (MIT, 2013) draw attention to the fact that the largest economies are increasingly driven by needs for innovative solutions created to satisfy a myriad of problems faced by manufacturers in scaling up ideas and education is influenced by these needs.

U.S.-based manufacturing is especially challenged due to the downsizing and hollowing out of the research and development (R&D) divisions of most large companies that has been occurring since the 1970s. A need exists for creative, innovative, and entrepreneurial people to tackle the existing problems encountered when ideas evolve from the drawing board to the factory floor and then on to the consumer in ways that can compete with similar products made in countries where people work for five dollars a day.

Corporations and small and medium-sized businesses that once researched, designed, developed, and manufactured products in-house have since stripped themselves down in many cases to design and sales operations and shifted the other aspects of manufacturing and research overseas. Known as "vertically-articulated corporations" (MIT, 2013, p. 25), these businesses were once one-stop-shops for the research, development, manufacturing, and sales for new products. People could start their careers in low-level positions and work their way up the various levels and divisions of the corporation.

The opportunities for personal and economic growth within vertically articulated businesses drove employees' pursuit of higher levels of education with the promise of promotion through the various divisions of the corporation. Whereas nineteenth-century skills built the post–World War II vertically articulated industrial economy, enabling people to pursue college education, it is now the competencies that are difficult to outsource to five-dollar-a-day countries, the competencies of creativity, innovation, and entrepreneurship, that set the bar for economic excellence and success in the global society.

The changed structural landscape of corporations was not a result of a reduction or lack of quality in public education output. The changes in corporate R&D behavior resulted from changes to tax, labor, industrial, and monetary policies at the state, national, and international levels (Pierce and Schott, 2012). Offshoring certain jobs to countries like Bangladesh, China, Pakistan, India, Vietnam, Thailand, and Mexico had more to do with policies developed at the World Bank, World Trade organization, and International

Monetary Fund and trade agreements like the North American Free Trade Agreement (NAFTA) and the Trans-Pacific Partnership (TPP), than a TIMSS or PISA science ranking (Pierce and Schott, 2012; Prestowitz, 2012, 2013).

The International Institute for Management Development (IMD, 2004) described the corporate offshoring practices in the United States as something akin to labor exploitation:

> For every dollar invested in the US, four dollars are invested by American enterprises abroad. Competitiveness has so far thrived on exploiting low cost opportunities around the world. Asia is attracting 60% of the investments going to developing countries. China has become the first recipient of direct investment and the 4th largest exporter of manufactured goods in the World. The US balance of trade is plunging to a staggering deficit of $581 billion dollars. However, about half of the imports entering the US are actually American products, manufactured abroad by American corporations and shipped back to the US.

The IMD (2004) report paints a picture of large U.S. corporations scouring the globe for low-cost manufacturing. Although the products are envisioned and designed in the United States, corporations are increasingly manufacturing and/or assembling the products elsewhere and shipping them back to the United States for consumers to buy. In essence, the U.S. consumer becomes the executioner of U.S. manufacturing and assembling by purchasing products from corporations that exploit pools of cheap labor around the globe. Policy makers in the United States euphemistically call the practice of offshoring jobs *free trade* and *global competitiveness*.

Because a lot of the R&D once housed in vertically articulated corporations shifted from the corporate sector to the university, government, and offshore sectors, it is now increasingly more difficult for small, and medium-sized innovative businesses to secure solutions for problems associated with in-house high-technology manufacturing and production (MIT, 2013). The R&D supports for product development and manufacturing that used to be part of the U.S. corporate landscape are no longer available in large quantities due to offshoring from free-trade policy making (Crotty, 2003; Schram, 2015).

Consequently, employers of small- and medium-sized innovative businesses need employees who come to the marketplace ready to demonstrate creative, innovative, and entrepreneurial competencies (MIT, 2013). They can no longer provide or are no longer willing to play a collaborative role in the training of employees that was a hallmark of corporate America decades ago. Corporations are no longer investing much in the way of monetary expenditures, time, or resources in employee development on innovative competencies. They search the world for labor stocks that possess them at the cheapest prices and attract or extract what is needed.

The United States Is Already There

Fortunately, due in part to its long history of local control of public education, the U.S. education system influences the development of unstandardized individuals, in large numbers. I draw upon a quote by Pericles (431 BC), made as part of his *Funeral Speech for the Athenian War Dead*, in which he stated, "We do not imitate the laws of neighboring countries. On the contrary, we are a model to others." This section presents an argument that the United States is already the world leader in creativity, innovation, and entrepreneurship and it has the largest supply of individuals with those competencies. It is the rest of the world that is trying to catch up.

The WEF, located in Geneva, Switzerland, is an international organization committed to free-market policy making. According to the WEF website (2016), the organization has the following characteristics and ideas:

- "International Organization for Public-Private Cooperation to shape the global, regional, national and industry agendas.
- Engages political, business, academic and other leaders of society in collaborative efforts to improve the state of the world. Together with other stakeholders, it works to define challenges, solutions and actions, always in the spirit of global citizenship.
- Strives in all its efforts to demonstrate entrepreneurship in the global public interest while upholding the highest standards of governance."

As such, the WEF maintains an annual ranking of global competitiveness, for over 130 economies, known as the Global Competitiveness Index or the GCI (WEF, 2015). The index is composed of "12 Pillars of Competitiveness" that align with the free-market ideology and view of global competitiveness (WEF, 2014). It is a similar ideology and view of global competitiveness that proponents of standardization speak of when they issue their dire warning that students in China are coming to take away U.S. jobs (Butcher, 2015).

The pillars of the GCI are (1) institutional environment, (2) infrastructure, (3) macroeconomic environment, (4) health and primary education, (5) higher education and training, (6) goods market efficiency, (7) labor market efficiency, (8) financial market development, (9) technological readiness, (10) market size, (11) business sophistication, and (12) innovation. The WEF calculates the overall GCI ranking from an average score of the 12 pillars and also provides individual rankings for each pillar.

The United States is consistently one of the most competitive economies in the world according the GCI. For example, since 1999, the United States has been the most globally competitive nation on the planet according to the WEF (WEF, 2016). The U.S. economy has ranked in the top three of the over

130 world economies included in the WEF rankings for twelve of the sixteen years from 1999 to 2015 (WEF, 2015). It is consistently the most competitive economy, in free-market terms, according to the WEF rankings.

The IMD also produces an annual ranking of global competitiveness for the fifty-five to sixty-one economies it includes in its ratings. The IMD releases the *World Competitiveness Rankings* yearly. According to IMD researchers, the global competitiveness of the nations in its sample is determined by the following general methods (2016):

- The ability of nations to create and maintain an environment in which enterprises can compete.
- We assume that wealth creation takes place primarily at enterprise level (whether private or state owned)—this field of research is called: "competitiveness of enterprises."
- Enterprises operate in a national environment which enhances or hinders their ability to compete domestically or internationally—this field of research is called: "competitiveness of nations" and is covered in our research.
- Our methodology thus divides the national environment into four main factors: (a) Economic Performance, (b) Government Efficiency, (c) Business Efficiency, (d) Infrastructure.

As with the WEF, the IMD focuses on global competitiveness and economic strength of nations through innovation, entrepreneurship, and profitability of businesses based on free-market principles. The IMD (2015) authors stated:

> Business efficiency focuses on the extent to which the national environment encourages enterprises to perform in an innovative, profitable and responsible manner. It is assessed through indicators related to productivity such as the labor market, finance, management practices and the attitudes and values that characterize the business environment.

Based on the IMD vision of global competitiveness, the United States was the strongest, most globally competitive economy in the world in 2015 (IMD, 2015). The IMD researchers ranked the U.S. economy first in the world nineteen times out of twenty in the years from 1996 to 2015.

An argument exists that the free-market agenda is inherently inhumane and strips the general public of important government services like school and health care and there is evidence that the argument has merit (e.g., Mullen, Samier, Brindley, English, and Carr, 2013). But the point made with the information presented thus far is that the U.S. economy is viewed by organizations that espouse free markets and global competitiveness as the most globally competitive on the planet, and has been for a long time. According to international organizations that monitor global competitiveness, the United States already possesses the global competitiveness advantage that proponents of standardizing public education claim it lacks.

DOWNSTREAM INDICATORS

The WEF and IMD represent two high-profile international organizations that track national global competitiveness in the innovation economy. Their rankings are important indicators of macroeconomic strength, but there are other indicators that provide glimpses of the influence of education's long-term outcomes of creativity, innovation, and entrepreneurship. Those are the attributes espoused by the multinational business community as necessary to drive and nurture an innovation economy well into 2050. Scientific research outputs are important indicators of innovation and creativity and precursors to the design and development of goods and services that drive an innovation economy.

Scientific Papers and Citations

Some indicators of high-quality and innovative scientific research and output are the numbers of scientific papers produced by a country overall and in specific fields like physics and chemistry. Thompson Reuters is one of the largest organizations that track national output of scientific papers. They compile longitudinal statistics at the country level that can be used as indicators of scientific innovation. Generally the Thompson Reuters reports cover 10 years of data. The statistics used in this section on papers and citations are the most updated available as of the time of this publication.

Perhaps the most comprehensive indicator of overall scientific output in terms of research and publications is the *Top 20 Countries in All Fields 2001–2011* report by Thompson Reuters (2011a). The United States ranked first with 3,049,666 scientific publications followed by the Peoples Republic of China (China) with 836,255 and Germany with 784,316. Japan ranked fourth and England was fifth. But the shear amount of papers alone is not the only measure of quality and innovation. Citations, or how often others reference and use a scientific paper, are perhaps more important.

Citations of scientific papers represent the level of acceptance and value of research and innovation put forth in scientific papers. It is a marker of quality. The more frequently a scientific paper is cited, the more frequently the ideas are being used and a higher frequency of citations signifies greater value of the ideas being cited. Once again, the United States was the world leader in citations of scientific papers with 48,862,100; more than four times that of second place Germany with 10,518,133 and third place England with 10,508,202. Japan and France were fourth and fifth and China was seventh (Thompson Reuters, 2011a).

The rankings for the *Top 20 Countries in Physics 1997–2007* for scientific papers and citations are similar to the citations rankings for the overall scientific papers cited above. The United States was first with 218,045 papers and 2,719,244 citations or 12.47 citations per paper. Japan was second with papers at 117,017 and third in citations with 899,691 whereas Germany was third with publications at 104,592 papers and second with citations at 1,100,855. China was fourth with papers at 86,679 but eighth with citations at 371,287 or 4.28 citations per paper (Thompson Reuters, 2008a).

The United States is also home to the majority of the top chemists in the world. As of 2010, 18 of the top 20 chemists, as determined by citation impact, were based in the United States (Thompson Reuters, 2011b). Many of the top 100 chemists were based in the United States and their work represents the vast majority of scientific publications and citations in the field of chemistry worldwide.

The results for scientific output in the sciences are interesting because of the constant drumbeat of failure sold to the U.S. public by some education bureaucrats and public education pundits. The rankings of high-quality scientific papers and citations contradict the aggregate U.S. rankings on all international tests of science. The results from the Thompson Reuters data are in direct opposition to the dire warnings of scientific collapse of the United States at the hands of the public school system. The U.S. public has sustained a steady diet of warnings about the need to "reform" public education to improve scientific output since the launch of *Sputnik 1*, yet scientific publications are at an all-time high.

Surely, given the monsoon of criticism about the state of math achievement for U.S. students, the United States cannot dominate the world in publications and citations in terms of mathematics papers, or could it? The mainstream media and proponents of curriculum and achievement standards consistently point to lagging U.S. mathematics achievement on international tests as a reason to support standardization programs (e.g., Green, 2014; Leef, 2013; Ryan, 2013).

According to the latest statistics regarding the top 20 countries in mathematics research, the United States ranks first in papers, citations, and citations per paper with 65,830, 268,096, and 4.07, respectively (Thompson Reuters, 2008b). The second- and third-place countries, France and Germany, had about a third and a quarter of that output, respectively. In fact, the combined output for France and Germany does not match that of the United States. China is 16th in terms of citations per paper.

Utility Patents

Scientific publications and citations are important indirect markers of long-term education output and innovative and creative thinking. Utility patents, sometimes known as innovation patents, represent another marker of innovation, creativity, and entrepreneurship at the national level (Thompson Reuters, 2014). The United States Patent and Trade Office (2013) defined utility patents as a patent "issued for the invention of a new and useful process, machine, manufacture, or composition of matter, or a new and useful improvement thereof." Utility patents are viewed as a primary proxy for innovation and a driver of innovation by many in the corporate community. But not all patents are created equal: Think, a breakthrough cancer-fighting drug versus a new bobble-head doll. The cancer drug required a utility, or innovation patent, whereas the bobble-head, although fun, used a lower-level, non-innovative type of a patent.

According to Bruce Nolop, the former Chief Financial Officer of Pitney Bowes and ETrade, in a *Wall Street Journal* interview on May 16, 2013, more innovation patents bring more corporate profits. "First, patents produce higher and more certain investment returns from innovation, effectively ensuring and magnifying the first-mover advantage and helping to justify sustained investments in R&D." Nolop also explained how the number of patents is a useful data point for tracking overall innovation and for planning corporate strategy. Nolop stated, "Second, patents create a scorecard for measuring innovation. The number of patents often serves as a quantifiable metric in setting corporate objectives and facilitates comparisons with competitors and industry benchmarks."

Rossbeth Moss Kanter from the Harvard Business School, explained in the same May 16, 2013, *Wall Street Journal* interview, that innovation patents beget more innovation. Kanter stated, "The ability to own a discovery and reap rewards from the investment in that unique invention or concept encourages innovation." Nolop's and Kanter's comments represent the overall view of the importance of innovation patents within the business community and affirm their usefulness as one metric from which to judge the overall innovative output of a country.

The U.S. Patent and Trademark Office (USPTO) is arguably the most competitive and quality-driven patent and trademark office in the world. Along with the Japanese and European Patent Offices, the USPTO grants patents for some of the most innovative ideas in the world. It is more difficult to receive a patent award from the USPTO than most other patent offices. When contrasted with the reported quality issues with the Chinese Patent System, it is clear that not all patents are created equal, nor are the review processes used at each patent office (Lin, 2014). Patents granted from the USPTO, Japanese Patent Office (JPO), and European Patent Office (EPO) represent the world's top innovations.

The United States has outcompeted the world in utility patents awarded in the top patent offices for over 50 years (USPTO, 2015a; 2015b). In 1965, the year after U.S. students ranked next to last on the FIMS, and eight years after the launch of the Sputnik I satellite by the Soviet Union, the United States ranked first in utility patents with 72,317 compared to 22,312 for the rest of the world (USPTO, 2015a). The United States ranked first in total patents granted in 2014 with 158,713 compared to 167,326 for the rest of the world. China was granted 7,291 total patents in 2014 (USPTO, 2015b). The U.S patent output shows no signs of slowing down.

Utility patents in many instances lead to products and services that drive the innovation economy and overall economic competitiveness. Utility patents are the canary in the innovation coal mine. If the United States was becoming globally less competitive, as claimed by some proponents of standardization since Sputnik I or the release of *A Nation at Risk* report in 1983 (NCEE, 1983), should there have been substantially less utility patents awarded to the United States since 1983? Conversely, the rest of the world, and specifically the countries that proponents of standardization claim are the most important competitors to the United States, should have been awarded substantially more utility patents than the United States. Yet, the United States has maintained dominance in the area of utility patents since the 1960s.

Nobel Prizes

Another long-term indicator of creativity and innovation are Nobel Prizes in the sciences and medicine. The Nobel Prizes in chemistry, physics, and medicine represent global acceptance and recognition of some of the most innovative and creative works in those areas. The work done by recipients in many cases represents the outcome of a lifetime of education pursuit. The United States has dominated Nobel Prizes in the sciences and medicine since the 1970s (Redovich, 2005). When that fact is raised during public presentations there are sometimes people who challenge the statement and counter with the response that the dominance by the United States was a remnant of the space race of the 1960s and 1970s and that many winners are foreign born and educated. Both points are wrong.

First, not only has the United States dominated Nobel Prizes in the sciences and medicine since the 1960s and 1970s, it continues to do so in the new millennium. U.S. physicists won 22 of the 45 Nobel Prizes awarded from 2000 to 2015. The next most successful country is Japan with six, followed by Russia and Germany with four each. Physicists from the U.K. were awarded three and France has won two Nobel Prizes in physics during the 16 years from 2000 to 2015. Physicists from China, and Belgium gained one prize each from 2000 to 2015.

The results are similar for Nobel Prizes in chemistry with U.S. scientists winning the majority and more than any other country with 24 of 38 prizes from 2000 to 2015. Japan gained four and Israeli scientists won three during that same time period. German and U.K. scientists won two and France, China, and New Zealand each were awarded one prize.

U.S. scientists rank first in Nobel Prizes for medicine, winning 19 out of 41 from 2000 to 2015. The U.K. comes the closest to challenging U.S. superiority with nine, followed by Japan and France with two each. In essence, the rest of the world combined out-produced the United States by only three awards in 16 years. The U.S. domination of Nobel Prizes is increasing, not decreasing. For example, Redovitch (2005) reported that U.S scientists won 41 prizes from 1979 to 1989, or 3.72 per year. Contrast that with the totals for 2000–2015 in which U.S. scientists have won 65 Nobel Prizes in 16 years or 4.06 per year during the time period.

Second, since 2003, 60 percent of the U.S. award winners were graduates of U.S. public schools (NASSP, 2013). In addition, foreigners who are not U.S. citizens but win a prize while working in the United States are counted as winners of their native countries (Redovich, 2005). U.S. Nobel Prize awards are not the result of a multitude of foreign educated scientists. U.S. scientists are not resting on their laurels from the space race. They are leading the world and no other country is close to catching them.

Nonstandard

Because the majority of patents and Nobel Prizes are granted to individuals or teams working in universities or companies, most recipients are aged 25 or older. In the case of Nobel Prizes, almost all the U.S. winners have been substantially older than 25. There are cases when someone younger than 25 receives a patent, but given that most utility patents are granted to working age people, the vast majority of the recipients are at least 25 years old. As of 2015, adults aged 25 or more attended public schools that were much less standardized and in many cases unstandardized in that standards were developed locally, yet those people are not being outcompeted. They are leading the world in scientific creativity and innovation. This fact is often overlooked or covered up by proponents of standardization.

Patent recipients in the United States were part of an American public school system of vast curricular diversity. The same can be said for the people writing the academic papers that receive all the citations and those people that eventually go on to win a Nobel Prize. Their achievements are in many ways products of, or at least influenced, by an unstandardized or less standardized education system.

INDICES OF CREATIVITY, INNOVATION, AND ENTREPRENEURSHIP

Creativity

The Martin Institute of Prosperity has published the Global Creativity Index since 2004. A recent index (i.e., 2015) provided rankings for 139 of the world's countries, including all the industrialized countries that make up the Organisation for Economic Co-operation and Development (OECD) members and partner countries. The index also includes the 19 members of the G20 group of nations. All the countries that many consider the United States' "competitors" are ranked by the index.

Researchers from the Institute compiled data from 2010 to 2014 relative to each country covering the following areas of creativity: economic, social, and cultural (Martin Prosperity Institute, 2015). The Institute's researchers used three categories to describe creativity: (a) technology, (b) talent, and (c) tolerance. Sub-domains within each category receive a coefficient rating, and each category receives a coefficient calculation; all three categories are used to arrive at an overall creativity coefficient for a country.

For example, within the Technology category, there were the sub-domains of (a) Global R&D Investment, (b) Global Researchers, and (c) Global Innovation. Those sub-domains created a coefficient for the Technology category. Within the Talent category there were the sub-domains of (a) Human Capital and (b) Creative Class. Those two sub-domains combine to represent the Talent Index. Tolerance is developed from (a) Tolerance toward Ethnic and Racial Minorities and (b) Tolerance toward Gays and Lesbians. They combined to make an overall Tolerance coefficient. A complete description of the methodology used can be found online starting on page 36 of the report (Martin Prosperity Institute, 2015).

The ratings from each of the three categories—technology, talent, and tolerance—are then added and averaged for an overall Creativity score. Scores are reported as a coefficient with the least creative country receiving an index score of 0.020 and the most creative, a score of 0.923. The maximum possible score is 1.000 and the lowest possible score is 0.000.

The United States ranked 2nd in overall Global Creativity in 2015 behind Australia. Other prominent members of the G20 lagged far behind. Italy was 21st, Japan 28th, South Korea 31st, Russia 38th, China 62nd, and India 99th. The United States ranked 3rd in Creative Talent behind Australia and Iceland. Somewhat surprisingly, given the cascade of negative comments toward the quality of U.S. public school achievement and concern of a advertised lag of global achievement, the United States ranked 2nd in the world in the category Educational Attainment necessary to turn creativity into economic output. South Korea ranked 1st (Martin Prosperity Institute, 2015). Apparently, the results from the GCI suggest that whatever gaps exist when students take their annual state standardized tests or PISA or TIMSS tests disappear later.

Creativity as measured by the Global Creativity Index has a positive association with economic strength as measured by the GCI calculated by the WEF. The relationship between creativity and economic strength and competitiveness, as measured by the GCI indices, is positive, and strong at 0.75. Similarly, the Global Creativity Index had a positive, moderate correlation of 0.65 with overall gross domestic product (GDP), another indicator of economic strength (Martin Prosperity Institute, p. 25). The PISA results do not correlate to those indicators for the G20 nations (Tienken and Tramaglini, 2017).

Innovation

The Global Innovation Index (GII) is another multilayered, multifactor, index used to rank the innovative capacity and output of nations (Cornell University, INSEAD, and WIPO, 2015). The index includes rankings for 142 countries. The overall GII is an average derived from the Innovation Efficiency Ratio (IER). IER is made up of the results from two subindices: Innovation Input and Innovation Output. Innovation Input is derived from five categories: (a) Institutions, (b) Human Capital and Research, (c) Infrastructure, (d) Market Sophistication, and (e) Business Sophistication. Innovation Output has two categories: (a) Knowledge and Technology Outputs and (b) Creative Outputs. Chapter 1 of the report, which can be found online, contains a complete description of the methodology used to determine the results (Cornell University, INSEAD, and WIPO, 2015).

The total of seven categories that form the Innovation Input and Innovation Output indicators each contain three factors for a total of 21 factors. Final scores for countries can range from 0–100. The highest score reported in 2015 was 68.30 for Switzerland and the lowest score was 7.20 for Togo. The average for the index was 37.01. The United States ranked fifth with a score of 60.10 and China ranked 28th with a score of 47.47. The Republic of Korea ranked 14th, Japan 19th, and Russia 48th.

The United States ranked first in the world on the sub-metric of innovation quality. The innovation quality ranking on the GII corresponds to the U.S. leadership in the area of innovation patents and is a confirmation that the United States is creating some of the highest quality innovations in the world. The United States ranked 2nd on University/Industry collaboration to drive innovation and 4th in overall Knowledge and Technology Outputs.

Entrepreneurship

Entrepreneurship can be considered an indirect indication of innovation and creativity. The Global Entrepreneurship Index (GEI), developed and implemented by the Global Entrepreneurship and Development Institute (GEDI), provides measures of entrepreneurial activities for 130 countries by collecting data at the individual and institutional levels. The authors of GEI provide a methodology to define entrepreneurship in quantitative ways to describe how much entrepreneurial capacity the majority of the countries in the world have and how much is operationalized (Acs, Szerb, and Autio, 2015). The authors measure entrepreneurship as the intersection of attitudes, actions, and aspirations.

Like the Global Creativity Index and the GII, the GEI is composed of sub-indexes for each of the three areas of entrepreneurship measured: (a) entrepreneurial attitudes, (b) entrepreneurial action, and (c) entrepreneurial aspirations. The three subindices are created from 34 factors related to individual and institutional attributes that facilitate and support entrepreneurship. Data are collected from over 15 different sources and includes approximately 20 variables. Results are reported on a scale of 0–100 with 100 representing the country with the most entrepreneurial activities. An explanation of the intricacies of the index and the calculation equation used can be found in chapter 5 of the official report that is accessible online (Acs, Szerb, and Autio, 2015).

The United States ranked first in the world out of 130 countries in overall entrepreneurship on the 2015 index, as it did on the 2014 index. The U.S. score of 85.00 was the highest score ever recorded on the index. Canada, Australia, the U.K., and Sweden rounded out the top five. The Republic of Korea ranked 28th with a score of 54.10, Japan ranked 33rd, Italy was 49th, China was 61st with a score of 36.40, and Russia ranked 70th.

The GEI also includes rankings for three sub-indexes: (a) Entrepreneurial Attitudes, (b) Entrepreneurial Abilities, and (c) Entrepreneurial Aspirations. The GEI authors (Acs, Szerb, and Autio, 2015) described key aspects of Entrepreneurial Attitudes as:

> The benchmark individuals are those who can recognize valuable business opportunities and have the skills to exploit them; who attach high status to entrepreneurs; who can bear and handle start-up risks; who know other entrepreneurs personally (i.e., have a network or role models); and who can generate future entrepreneurial activities. (p. 21)

Entrepreneurial Abilities are defined as:

> Start-ups in the medium- or high-technology sectors that are initiated by educated entrepreneurs, and launched because a person is motivated by an

> opportunity in an environment that is not overly competitive. Entrepreneurial abilities also refer to the equal participation of women in start-ups and other opportunities. (p. 21)

Entrepreneurial Aspirations are defined as:

> Early-stage entrepreneur's effort to introduce new products and/or services, develop new production processes, penetrate foreign markets, substantially increase their company's staff, and finance the business with formal and/or informal venture capital.

The United States ranked 1st in Entrepreneurial Attitudes, 2nd in Entrepreneurial Abilities behind Canada, and 1st in Entrepreneurial Aspirations.

Less Standardized

The target populations for the GCI, GII, and GEI were mostly adults aged 25 or older. In some cases the GEI used data from national and international indices that included people 18 to 65 years of age. Similar to the age ranges for writers of academic research, patent recipients, and Nobel Prize winners, the age ranges for the GCI, GII, and GEI are important to note because the overwhelming majority of people involved in the data collection processes for these indices attended school at times when public school was unstandardized or at least at times when schools had much looser standards for curriculum and output expectations.

Of course a handful of states like New York had curriculum standards and testing for a long time, many decades in fact. But overall, even New York's former system of standardization was not anything like the straitjacket of standards and testing imposed in 2016. There was always some slack in the system that allowed creativity and innovation to thrive, not just survive.

The results presented thus far in this chapter begin to challenge the notion that a heavily standardized curricular program, enforced with requirements for specific performance outputs, and enforced with a testing system that punishes educators will produce or foster more creativity and innovation than what already exists.

LACK OF QUALIFIED EMPLOYEES

When some students in education leadership graduate programs or members of the public hear the aforementioned statistics about competitiveness and innovation there are invariably rebuttals, masked as questions, along the lines of, "well, aren't most of those patents and high-tech engineering and development achievements from foreign workers that U.S. businesses have to hire because there are not enough qualified U.S. citizens to fill those positions?"

A congressional mandated process controls the importation of skilled labor into the United States. A key feature of the control process is the awarding of H-1B visas for advanced-skill workers. There is an annual cap, set by the U.S. Congress, on the number of H-1B visas that can be awarded. In 2015 Congress set that cap at 85,000 (The United States Citizenship and Immigration Service [USCIS], 2015). The USCIS (2015) provides an overview of the visa on its website:

> The H-1B visa has an annual numerical limit, or cap, of 65,000 visas each fiscal year. The first 20,000 petitions filed on behalf of beneficiaries with a U.S. master's degree or higher are exempt from the cap. Additionally, H-1B workers who are petitioned for or employed at an institution of higher education (or its affiliated or related nonprofit entities), a nonprofit research organization, or a government research organization are not subject to this numerical cap.

In past years Congress allowed more visas to be distributed but the overall count ranges based on congressional allocation. For example, President Bill Clinton's administration lobbied for and secured 115,000 visas in 1999 whereas the total has remained at approximately 85,000 under President Barack Obama. Considering that there were approximately 122 million people employed in the United States in September 2015, a 0.0009 percent allowance for highly specialized foreign workers seems reasonable (Statista, 2015).

Some claim the use of H-1B visas are necessary due to a failing U.S. education system that does not produce enough highly skilled employees and that the visas maintain a global competitiveness advantage for the United States (e.g., Giffi, Dollar, Drew, McNelly, Carrick, and Gangula, 2015; Yu, 2007). The data presented in this chapter thus far refute that claim, but there exists other evidence that the clamoring for more H-1B visas on the part of corporations and some members of the U.S. Congress is not about a lack of skilled employees. Rutgers University Professor Hal Salzman testified before a Senate Judiciary Committee in 2015. Salzman stated there are more than enough high-quality candidates in the science and technology fields available within the United States (Immigration Reforms Needed to Protect Skilled American Workers: Hearings before the Judiciary Committee, Senate, 114th Congress, 2015a).

> The U.S. supply of top performing graduates is large and far exceeds the hiring needs of the STEM industries, with only half of new STEM graduates finding

jobs in a STEM occupation (and only a third of all STEM graduates in the workforce holding a STEM job).

As Professor Salzman stated, the use of H-1B visas to fill high-tech positions is not always used because of a shortage of high-skilled U.S. citizens. The H-1B visa is not as widely used by U.S. companies as some might claim. Foreign-owned companies from India make up the largest users of H-1B visas. The majority of the "Top 10" users of H-1B visas, 7/10, are Indian multinational companies that hire workers trained in India to work in their U.S. operations for lower wages than a similarly qualified U.S. citizen (MyVisaJobs, 2015). Infosys, Tata Consultancy Services, and Wipro, all Indian multinational corporations, were the top three users of H-1B visas.

In 2014 almost 86 percent of all H-1B visas were granted to Indian citizens and most of those people went to work in Indian companies whereas only 5 percent of visas went to Chinese nationals (Thibodeau and Machlis, 2015). Of course companies like Apple and Google use H-1B visas, as do some of the major accounting firms like Deloitte, but the majority of H-1B foreign workers are working for their countries' multinational corporations, not U.S.-based companies. In some cases those companies pay H-1B visa holders considerably less than the median salary paid to a similarly qualified U.S. citizen.

Greed Trumps the Facts

Consider that median salaries for Indian nationals working in India, in metropolitan areas like Bangalore, Mumbai, or Delhi, with masters and doctoral degrees is around 1.4 million rupees or $22,000 U.S. dollars (USD) a year. The median salary is around 1.6 million rupees, or $25,000 USD, for senior IT software engineers. The financial sector pays the most, with the median salary being around 2 million rupees, or $30,000 USD for people with masters and doctoral degrees in senior financial analysts positions (Payscale, 2015).

Contrast the salaries from Delhi, Mumbai, and Bangalore with a median salary for a senior software engineer working in New York City at $113,000 USD a year, or almost $78,000 USD a year for a senior financial analyst, living and commuting say about 40 minutes from New York City in a location like Edison, New Jersey, where the cost of living is less than in New York City (Bureau of Labor Statistics [BLS], 2015; Payscale, 2015). Clearly the salary differences are substantially in favor of the non-H-1B employee. Non-H-1B employees are paid more. According to congressional testimony to the U.S. Senate Judiciary Committee in March 2015, some foreign companies are using the H-1B visa as a way to pay lower wages than they would if they hired equally qualified U.S. citizens (Immigration Reforms Needed to Protect Skilled American Workers, 2015b).

Salaries for H-1B visas are governed by congressional guidelines and those guidelines require holders of H-1B visa to be paid the prevailing wage. However, the H-1B salary guidelines allow for varying prevailing wages based on skill level and the company in which the H-1B visa holder works determines the skill level and hence the pay level. For example, for a physicist with a doctoral degree working in the White Plains, New York, area the H-1B salary can range from a minimum of $52,749 a year to maximum of approximately $143,000 a year depending on the level of qualification (Foreign Labor and Certification Data Center [FLC], 2016).

H-1B visa holders can receive one of four possible wages based on experience and skill level (United States Department of Labor, 2009). Level 1 is considered entry level and represents the lowest prevailing wage for a job category. In the example of the physicist, Level 1 would receive approximately $52,749 a year. Level 2 is considered qualified, meaning the H-1B holder possesses the minimum education or experience for the job. Level 3 is considered experienced and generally includes managerial positions or lead positions, like Lead Physicist, and the salary is approximately $113,000 a year. Level 4 employees are considered fully competent, have management and/or supervisory experiences, and the salary is approximately $143,000 a year.

The rough mean salary for the H-1B physicist is approximately $98,165 and median salary approximately $97,500. Of course the salaries presented are rough estimates based on aggregate data and governed by geographic cost of living factors, but they provide some benchmarks from which to make comparisons. The BLS places the mean annual wage for a non-H-1B physicist at $117,300 and the median salary at $109,600. Both salaries are considerably higher than the H-1B prevailing mean (BLS, 2015). The average top salary for a non-H-1B physicist is approximately $215,000 a year.

The prevailing wages for the H-1B visa holders are determined by the potential employer entering data into a federal worksheet. The worksheet calculates values and produces a prevailing wage. The employer can also elect to use a preset determination based on federal guidelines. The large difference in prevailing wages makes it more cost effective for companies to lower their wage costs by hiring H-1B visa holders. In the physicist example, a company can claim that their candidate possesses Level 1 or Level 2 skills and pay the physicist $52,749 instead of a higher salary the company would most likely have to pay a similarly qualified U.S. citizen.

The differences between the H-1B salary for a physicist and the non-H-1B physicist is sizable and the differences provide an incentive for corporations looking to cut costs to hire H-1B holders over U.S. citizens, not because of superior qualifications, but because of lower wages. Simply put, corporations that use H-1B visas to fill positions pay those employees less, on average, than they would have to pay equally qualified U.S. citizens (Harkinson, 2013).

In the cases of India or China, the physicist is earning perhaps $25,000–$40,000 in his or her home country, and thus the Level 1 salary is a large increase. Hence, the foreign scientists accept salaries that are lower than they would be if they were U.S. citizens. This salary scenario is not a hypothetical situation. There are examples of H-1B visa abuses documented in mainstream business magazines and other outlets. For instance, Infosys, the Indian multinational technology company, paid the U.S. government and Texas a combined total of 34 million dollars to settle a visa fraud case in which the company was accused of preferential employment of H-1B visa holders over similarly or more highly qualified U.S. citizens, and paying those visa holders less (Schoenberg, McLaughlin and Korosec, 2013).

In some cases qualified U.S. workers are laid off in favor of less qualified, cheaper, H-1B holders and asked to train their replacements (Lam, 2015). Walt Disney Parks and Resorts in Florida provided such an example. The company replaced approximately 250 IT workers with H-1B holders from India. The displaced Disney workers were mandated to train their replacements or they would not receive their severance packages (Lam, 2015). The same scenario took place at a Connecticut location of the pharmaceutical giant Pfizer in 2013 in which U.S. employees were replaced with H-1B visa holders (Harkinson, 2013). The displaced U.S. workers were coerced into training their H-1B replacements.

Not only are H-1B visa holders paid less in many situations, they are not always highly skilled or more skilled than U.S. workers. Data suggest that most H-1B visa holders at the top six companies that use the visa process to hire foreign labor have only a bachelor's degree (Hira, 2015; Immigration Reforms Needed to Protect Skilled American Workers, 2015b). The percentage of visa holders with bachelor's degrees ranged from 62 to 86 at the top six H-1B employers. Many don't consider a BA degree to represent a "highly skilled" employee. BA degrees are a basic requirement for most entry-level corporate jobs.

The data on degree status and the fact that many H-1B holders need to be trained by the U.S. workers they are brought in at a lower salary to replace suggest that the majority of people employed with H-1B visas in high-technology IT or finance positions are less skilled and less qualified than the U.S. workers they are displacing (Matloff, 2013; Immigration Reforms Needed to Protect Skilled American Workers, 2015b). There is more to the calls from corporations like Infosys, Google, and Microsoft for more H-1B visas than meets the eye. The data suggest that for some corporations the H-1B has become a type of perverted corporate welfare benefit to boost profits.

Although there might be isolated cases when a small amount of specialized labor is warranted, the data suggest the claims of unqualified U.S. workers are overstated and are being used to drive down wages and increase profits. Professor Salzman stated:

> The predominant function of IT guest-worker visa programs is to facilitate the offshoring of IT work—that is, the ability of firms to move IT work from the U.S. to offshore locations is highly dependent on their supply of H-1B and L visas for their companies. These are companies such as IBM, Accenture, Deloitte, Ernst & Young, as well as the internationally based firms such as Infosys, Wipro, and TCS. (Immigration Reforms Needed to Protect Skilled American Workers, 2015a)

It is important to have a global labor force. The cross-pollination of ideas, through the development and careful nurturing of a diverse labor force helps to bring about economic nimbleness. The diversity of the U.S. workforce is an important strength, and xenophobic rhetoric and policies should not be tolerated or encouraged. The examples of H-1B visa fraud were not used as a call to seal the borders in a mindless or racist attempt to insulate the United States from the outside world, but as yet more evidence that the claims and narratives being used by proponents of standardization that the United States lacks qualified labor and is losing competitiveness have serious flaws.

The calls by corporate leaders to expand the number of H-1B visas to 200,000 are unfounded if the reason given is a lack of qualified workers in the United States The United States consistently ranks in the Top 10 of all industrialized countries for worker productivity. The U.S. workforce is one of the most productive on the world. According to the OECD (2015), the U.S. workforce ranked 3rd in the industrialized world in productivity as measured by GDP per hour worked, behind Luxemburg and Norway. The U.S. workforce has been one of the most productive in the industrialized world since 1979 in terms of GDP per hour worked (BLS, 2012).

THE GRASS IS NOT GREENER

The data presented in this chapter suggest that the United States is a global leader in creativity, innovation, and entrepreneurship as measured by multiple indices and outputs. The U.S. worker is also one of the most productive workers in the world. Although there is always room for improvement, the data suggest that there is not a global competitiveness crisis in the United States in terms of the attributes influenced by education that drive the innovation economy.

The quality of the human resources to drive an innovation economy exists in the United States in great quantities and those human resources are highly productive. The human resources needed to scale up high-tech manufacturing already exist in the United States and overwhelming majority of the workforce was educated here. Again, consider that those human resources aged 25 or older were educated in a more unstandardized public education system, not the assembly-line edu-factory being imposed on the approximately 56 million students that attend public school daily in the United States.

Next Steps

The formally less standardized public education system did not fail. On the contrary, it helped to produce what some data suggest is one of the most innovative, creative, and entrepreneurial countries on the planet. The claims by proponents of standardization about waning competitiveness and a lack of highly skilled candidates are false. Don't believe the hype. But beyond the worn out arguments and weak data presented by proponents of standardization, the entire concept rests on failed philosophies and theories.

The next chapter presents a critique of some of the most common ideologies, philosophies, and theories that underlie standardization policies and practices. It is not an exhaustive review as this is not a textbook, but the review does provide a look into the underbelly of standardization and helps to explain why such policies and programs will never achieve their advertised promises.

REFERENCES

Acs, Z.J., Szerb, L., & Autio, E. (2015). *The global entrepreneurship index 2015.* Washington, DC: The Global Entrepreneurship and Development Institute. Retrieved from file:///Users/Sicilia/Downloads/Global-Entrepreneurship-Index-2015-for-web1.pdf.

Bureau of Labor Statistics. (2015). *Occupational employment and wages, May 2014.* 15–1133 Software developers. Author. Retrieved from http://www.bls.gov/oes/current/oes151133.htm.

Bureau of Labor Statistics. (2012). *Real GDP per hour worked by country 1960–2011.* Author. Retrieved from http://www.bls.gov/ilc/intl_gdp_capita_gdp_hour.htm#table03.

Butcher, S. (2015, July 9). Why outstanding Chinese students want your job in finance. *Efinancial Careers.* Retrieved from http://news.efinancialcareers.com/uk-en/215871/why-outstanding-chinese-students-want-your-job-in-finance/.

Cornell University, INSEAD, & WIPO. (2015). *The global innovation index 2015: Effective innovation policies for development. Fontainebleau, Ithaca, and Geneva.* Retrieved from https://www.globalinnovationindex.org/userfiles/file/reportpdf/gii-full-report-2015-v6.pdf.

Crotty, J. (2003). *The Neoliberal Paradox: The impact of destructive product market competition and impatient finance on Nonfinancial Corporations in the Neoliberal Era.* Political Economy Research Institute. Research Brief 2003–2005. Retrieved from http://core.ac.uk/download/pdf/6548878.pdf.

Foreign Labor and Certification Data Center [FLC]. (2016). *FLC wage results: Physicist.* Retrieved from http://www.flcdatacenter.com/OesQuickResults.aspx?code=19-2012&area=35644&year=16&source=1.

Giffi, C., Dollar, B., Drew, M., McNelly, J., Carrick, G., & Gangula, B. (2015). *The skills gap in U.S. manufacturing: 2015 and beyond.* Deloitte Development LLC and The Manufacturing Institute. Retrieved from http://www.themanufacturinginstitute.org/~/media/827DBC76533942679A15EF7067A704CD.ashx.

Green, E. (2014, July 23). Why do Americans stink at math? *The New York Times Magazine.* Retrieved from http://www.nytimes.com/2014/07/27/magazine/why-do-americans-stink-at-math.html?_r=0.

Harbison, F. & Myers, C. (Eds.). (1956). *Manpower and education.* New York: McGraw-Hill.

Harkinson, J. (2013, February 22). How H-1B visas are screwing the American worker. *Mother Jones.* Retrieved from http://www.motherjones.com/politics/2013/02/silicon-valley-h1b-visas-hurt-tech-workers.

Hira, R. (2015, February 19). New data show how firms like Infosys and Tata abuse H-1B program. *Economic Policy Institute.* Retrieved from http://www.epi.org/blog/new-data-infosys-tata-abuse-h-1b-program/.

Immigration Reforms Needed to Protect Skilled American Workers. Hearings before the Judiciary Committee, Senate, 114th Congress. (2015a). (Testimony of Hal Salzman.) Retrieved from http://www.judiciary.senate.gov/imo/media/doc/03-17-15%20Salzman%20Testimony%20Updated.pdf.

Immigration Reforms Needed to Protect Skilled American Workers. Hearings before the Judiciary Committee, Senate, 114th Congress. (2015b). (Testimony of Jay Palmer, Jr.) Retrieved from http://www.judiciary.senate.gov/imo/media/doc/Palmer%20Testimony.pdf.

International Institute for Management Development [IMD]. (2016). *Methodology.* Author Lausanne, Switzerland. Retrieved from http://www.imd.org/wcc/research-methodology/.

International Institute for Management Development [IMD]. (2015). *IMD world competitiveness yearbook 2015.* Author. Retrieved from http://www.imd.org/news/IMD-releases-its-2015-World-Competitiveness-Ranking.cfm.

International Institute for Management Development [IMD]. (2004). *IMD world competitiveness yearbook 2004.* Lausanne, Switzerland.

Lam, B. (2015, June 18). America's mixed feelings about immigrant labor: Disney-layoff edition. *The Atlantic.* Retrieved from http://www.theatlantic.com/business/archive/2015/06/disney-h1b-visas-immigration-layoffs/396149/.

Leef, G. (2013, October 24). A key reason why American students do poorly. *Forbes.* Retrieved from http://www.forbes.com/sites/georgeleef/2013/10/24/a-key-reason-why-american-students-do-poorly/.

Lin, M. (2014, March 27). Patent quality in China. *IPWatchdog*. Retrieved from http://www.ipwatchdog.com/2014/03/27/patent-quality-in-china/id=48720/.

Martin Prosperity Institute. (2015). The global creativity index 2015. Author. Retrieved from http://martinprosperity.org/media/Global-Creativity-Index-2015.pdf.

Massachusetts Institute of Technology. (MIT). (2013). *Report of the MIT task force on innovation and production*. Author. Retrieved from http://web.mit.edu/press/images/documents/pie-report.pdf.

Matloff, N. (2013). Are foreign students the best and the brightest? *Economic Policy Institute*. Retrieved from http://www.epi.org/publication/bp356-foreign-students-best-brightest-immigration-policy/.

Mullen, C.A., Samier, E.A., Brindley, S., English, F.W., & Carr, N.K. (2013). An epistemic frame analysis of neoliberal culture and politics in the US, UK, and UAE. *Interchange, 43*(3), 187–228.

MyVisaJobs.com. (2015). *2014 H1B visa reports*. Author. Retrieved from http://www.myvisajobs.com/Reports/2014-H1B-Visa-Sponsor.aspx.

National Association of Secondary School Principals (NASSP). (2013). What's right about U.S. public schools. *Principal.org*. Retrieved from http://www.principalspr.org/whatsright.html.

National Commission on Excellence in Education. (1983). *A nation at risk*. Washington, DC: U.S. Department of Education.

Organisation for Economic Co-operation and Development [OECD]. (2015). *OECD.stat: Level of GDP per capita and productivity*. OECD. Retrieved from http://stats.oecd.org/Index.aspx?DataSetCode=PDB_LV.

Payscale. (2015). *Master of business administration (MBA), finance degree average salary*. Retrieved from http://www.payscale.com/research/IN/Degree=Master_of_Business_Administration_(MBA)%2c_Finance/Salary#by_City.

Pierce, J.R. & Schott, P.K. (2012). *The surprisingly swift decline of U.S. manufacturing employment.* Yale School of Management and National Bureau of Economic Research. Retrieved from http://economics.yale.edu/sites/default/files/schott-09-oct-2013.pdf.

Pericles. (431 BC). *Funeral speech for the Athenian War dead.* Retrieved from http://www.rjgeib.com/thoughts/athens/athens.html.

Prestowitz, C. (2013, May 9). Triumph of the mercantilists. *Foreign Policy*. Retrieved from http://prestowitz.foreignpolicy.com/posts/2013/05/09/triumph_of_the_mercantilists.

Prestowitz, C. (2012, February 22). GE's competitiveness charade. *Foreign Policy*. Retrieved from http://prestowitz.foreignpolicy.com/posts/2012/02/22/ges_competitiveness_charade5.

Redovich, D. (2005). The big con in education. Why must all high school graduates be prepared for college? *iUniverse*. Bloomington, IN.

Ryan, J. (2013, December 3). American schools vs. the world: Expensive, unequal, and bad at math. *The Atlantic*. Retrieved from http://www.theatlantic.com/education/archive/2013/12/american-schools-vs-the-world-expensive-unequal-bad-at-math/281983/.

Schram, S.F. (2015). *The return of ordinary capitalism: Neoliberalism, precarity, occupy*. Oxford, UK: Oxford University Press.

Schoenberg, T., McLaughlin, D., & Korosec, T. (2013, October 31). Infosys settles with U.S. in visa fraud probe. *Bloomberg Business*. Retrieved from http://www.bloomberg.com/news/articles/2013-10-30/infosys-settles-with-u-s-in-visa-fraud-probe.

Statista. (2015, September). *Monthly number of full-time employees in the United States from September 2014 to September 2015 (in millions, unadjusted)*. Retrieved from http://www.statista.com/statistics/192361/unadjusted-monthly-number-of-full-time-employees-in-the-us/.

Thibodeau, P. & Machlis, S. (2015, August 10). With H-1B visa, diversity does not apply. *Computer World.* Retrieved from http://www.computerworld.com/article/2956584/it-outsourcing/with-h-1b-visa-diversity-doesnt-apply.html.

Thompson Reuters. (2014). *Derwent world patents index. 2014 state of innovation.* Author. Retrieved from http://ip.thomsonreuters.com/sites/default/files/2014 stateofinnovation.pdf.

Thompson Reuters. (2011a). *Top 20 countries in all fields 2001–2011.* Author. Retrieved from http://sciencewatch.com/articles/top-20-countries-all-fields-2001-august-31-2011.

Thompson Reuters. (2011b). *Top 20 Chemists 2000–2010.* Author. Retrieved from http://sciencewatch.com/articles/top-100-chemists-2000-2010.

Thompson Reuters. (2008a). *Top 20 countries in physics 1997–2007.* Author. Retrieved from http://sciencewatch.com/articles/top-20-countries-physics-1997-2007.

Thompson Reuters. (2008b). *Top 20 countries in mathematics 1998–2008.* Retrieved from http://sciencewatch.com/articles/top-20-countries-mathematics-1998-2008.

Tienken, C.H. & Tramaglini, T. (2017). International test rankings and student academic performance: It's the economy stupid. In D. Sharpes (Ed.), *Handbook of comparative and international education*. New York: Information Age Publishing.

Tramaglini, T.W. & Tienken, C.H. (2016). *Customized curriculum and high achievement in high poverty schools*. In C. Tienken & C. Mullen (Eds.), *Education policy perils: Tackling the tough issues* (pp. 75–101). Philadelphia, PA: Taylor Francis.

U.S. Citizenship and Immigration Services. (2015). *Understanding H-1B requirements* Retrieved from http://www.uscis.gov/eir/visa-guide/h-1b-specialty-occupation/understanding-h-1b-requirements.

United States Department of Labor. (2009). *Prevailing Wage determination policy guidance for nonagricultural immigration programs*. Retrieved from http://www.flcdatacenter.com/download/NPWHC_Guidance_Revised_11_2009.pdf.

U.S. Patent and Trademark Office [USPTO]. (2013). *Types of patents.* Author. Retrieved from http://www.uspto.gov/web/offices/ac/ido/oeip/taf/patdesc.htm.

U.S. Patent and Trademark Office [USPTO]. (2015a). *U.S. patent statistics chart calendar years 1963–2014.* Author. Retrieved from http://www.uspto.gov/web/offices/ac/ido/oeip/taf/us_stat.htm.

U.S. Patent and Trademark Office [USPTO]. (2015b). *All patents, all types 1990–2014.* Author. Retrieved from http://www.uspto.gov/web/offices/ac/ido/oeip/taf/apat.pdf.

Wall Street Journal. (2013, May 16) *The experts: Does the patent system encourage innovation?* Retrieved from http://www.wsj.com/articles/SB10001424127887323582904578487200821421958.

World Economic Forum [WEF]. (2016). *Reports*. Geneva, Switzerland. Author. Retrieved from http://www.weforum.org/reports.

World Economic Forum [WEF]. (2015). *The global competitiveness report 2015–2016*. Author. Retrieved from http://reports.weforum.org/global-competitiveness-report-2015-2016/.

World Economic Forum [WEF]. (2014). *The global competitiveness report 2014–2015*. Author. Retrieved from http://www3.weforum.org/docs/WEF_GlobalCompetitivenessReport_2014-15.pdf.

Yu, M.C. (2007, July 19). Beware the H-1B visa. *Bloomberg business. The debate room*. Retrieved from http://www.businessweek.com/debateroom/archives/2007/09/beware_the_h-1b_visa.html.

Chapter 4

Fatally Flawed Foundations

The theories and philosophies that proponents of standardization use to support their positions are diametrically opposed to the complementary functions of a free and democratic public school system and the skills and dispositions necessary for global economic competitiveness. The theories and philosophies that support standardization drive policies and practices that ultimately result in conformity, social immobility, and plutocracy.

Standardized and mechanistic education was implemented on a large scale before the turn of the twentieth century and up through the progressive era. The implementation of such a system resulted in abysmal high school graduation rates and low postsecondary participation. The percentage of students graduating high school stood at less than 17 percent in 1920 (Simon and Grant, 1965). College participation was reserved for a small elite minority.

Policy mandates that result in the standardization of curriculum, instruction, and assessment of students and educators derive support from the flawed anchor theory of performativity (Lyotard, 1984). Embedded within performativity are aspects of extreme behaviorism, the Essentialist philosophy of education, linguistic relativism, the Cult of Specificity, and an unyielding belief in meritocracy. The standardized theories and philosophies eschew the egalitarian spirit of public school that is necessary to maintain a participative and economically competitive democracy built on equity and social justice.

EGALITARIANISM

In its most basic sense, egalitarianism is an ideology that posits that everyone should be afforded equal treatment and equal access to a society's social mobility apparatus in order to lead a productive and sustaining life (Roemer, 1998). A comprehensive public education system is part of that apparatus. A spirit of egalitarianism promotes policies and practices that seek to develop a diversity of talents and value diversity as a positive attribute to be nurtured, not homogenized. An egalitarian system of public education received support early on in the United States from proponents like U.S. President Thomas Jefferson and Massachusetts educator Horace Mann. Both advocated for a public education system that, within the social confines of the times, unified diverse peoples, in the spirit of all people being created equal (Tienken, 2013).

Other champions of egalitarian policies, including philosopher-educator John Dewey, supported the concept of a unitary system of public education as a way to foster egalitarian principles and democracy in general. Dewey advocated for a public school system built upon a curricular foundation of socially conscious problem solving aimed at strengthening democracy. Dewey's conception of public education traveled across continents and later became the basis to Freier's problem-posing education (2000) in Brazil and democratic schooling movements in Italy prior to World War II. Dewey (1915; 1916) wrote that all citizens should have the right to participate actively and equally in the democratic governing of the nation and a democratic system of schooling was the best preparation for full participation.

Like Jefferson and Mann, Dewey (1916) was concerned about the transformation of the U.S. democracy into a plutocracy in which a wealthy and powerful minority controls the majority of the population through policies and programs based on the principles of social Darwinism and meritocracy. Social Darwinism is an ideology that suggests only the strongest individuals or most economically endowed should receive the maximum benefits of a system (Bannister, 1989).

Policies in K–12 education that exemplify social Darwinism include one-size-fits-all academic programs in which the child is made to fit a narrow, predetermined expectation of success. Academic tracking situations in which students cannot exit a track once placed in it and entrance and exit criteria for academic programs based on standardized test results that have been consistently demonstrated to discriminate against students of poverty are hallmarks of a standardized Darwinian education system. Social Darwinism is the antithesis of egalitarianism.

The devolution of democracy into plutocracy via the undercutting of egalitarian policies and practices was one concern of Dewey's. He advocated that the United States should have public structures, including a unitary public school system, to help prepare children for a participative democracy and guard against plutocracy. Dewey supported an expanded public school system where privileged and less privileged students worked and learned side-by-side, just as they would have to do after they entered into adult life

(Tanner and Tanner, 2007). As such, Dewey advocated for a diverse and flexible curriculum with opportunities to learn the skills and dispositions necessary for democratic participation in an uncertain future.

Egalitarianism at Work

Education policy and broader social policies based on egalitarian constructs might include provisions for structures, policies, and programs aimed at widening participation in quality education experiences as a means to increase broad democratic and economic participation and upward social mobility for all people. An egalitarian policy framework would seek to decrease or revise policies and practices that favor elite segments of a population such as the wealthiest citizens (Tienken, 2013).

Take for example, the practice in some states that allows publically funded specialty academic high schools, including magnet schools, charter schools, or selective vocational-technical academies to use standardized criteria to select students for enrollment or retention in the schools. Wealthier students most often meet the criteria for enrollment whereas the poorest students, second-language learners, or students with special needs are more often not enrolled in or they are more frequently exited from such programs. Many charter schools, specialty academies, selective vocational academies, and magnet schools have more homogenous student populations than their neighborhood schools, based on socioeconomics, race, prior academic achievement, second-language learners, or special needs categories (Frankenberg, 2011; Miron, Urschel, Mathis, and Tornquist, 2010; Tienken and Orlich, 2013).

Curriculum, instruction, and assessment policies and practices in an egalitarian unitary system would be developed and structured according to research-based principles (e.g., Dewey, 1902; Tanner and Tanner, 2007; Tyler, 1949) such as

- what has been demonstrated empirically and through evidence-based practice to best facilitate student academic, cognitive, and social development;
- the ways in which more students learn best based on democratic principles; and
- students, teachers, parents, and the larger community having collective input and involvement in curriculum development so that it reflects the current society and prepares students for an unknown future.

Egalitarian policies can help educators provide all students, regardless of race or class, access to quality education opportunities and facilitate the removal of obstacles to achieve universal education quality. A more egalitarian approach to publically funding specialty schools, charter schools, and magnet schools would first be to not allow such institutions to exist because they segregate the population and create elitist colonies. They are a danger to democracy and should be outlawed. A policy compromise based on egalitarian principles would be to make sure the demographics in those types of schools matched the demographics from the communities served or covered by the school and that those types of elitist schools were subjected to the same regulations placed on public schools.

It stands to reason that the aims of egalitarian education policies can only be fully realized if supported by wider egalitarian social policies, due to the close link between socioeconomic status, social capital, human capital, and student achievement in the United States (Sirin, 2005; Tienken, 2016). Just as the flower needs the rain and the poet needs the pain (Bon Jovi, Bryan, and Sambora, 1992), education policy needs broader participation by other societal supports, such as tax, housing, foreign, trade, industrial, and health policies, to facilitate upward economic growth for those students most displaced in a capitalistic global economy (Atkinson and Leigh, 2008; Hungerford, 2012). But an egalitarian mindset in policy making and implementation is a helpful tool regardless of whether other types of policies are in place.

ESSENTIALISM

The driving philosophical force behind many of the standardization programs is Essentialism. The calls for increased "rigor" or "academic excellence" based on a shallow pool of century-old static knowledge, or mastering a set of "core knowledge," or even the claim that global competitiveness can be increased by excelling at only a few subjects all have roots in Essentialism. Tanner and Tanner (2007, p. 198) provide what some consider the most complete overview of the philosophy and thus, an elongated description is not presented. Instead, some important characteristics of Essentialism that connect to standardization are discussed.

One education goal of Essentialism is to prepare students for the way the world is today. Preparation for the world as it currently exists signifies the use of a static curricular program driven by knowledge accumulation without care for knowledge discovery, knowledge evolution, knowledge innovation, or overall social progress. There is not a focus on the skills and dispositions necessary to cope with and thrive in an uncertain future. The focus on "today" results in a focus on what was known in the past to maintain the present societal caste structure.

A standardized collection of knowledge is the centerpiece of an Essentialist curricular program. Essentialism places value on remembering and imitating the collection of existing content knowledge and encountering that content in neatly prepackaged modules imposed by a bureaucratic apparatus for mass consumption, not critical evaluation. The imposed content exists without attention for the need to connect content to the child. Acquiring, storing, and cementing the knowledge and the culture of the ruling class are of utmost importance in the Essentialist philosophy.

Dewey (1938/1997) described the antistudent view of Essentialist education programs in the following terms:

> Ignore and minimize the child's individual peculiarities, whims, and experiences. They are what we need to get away from. . . . Sub-divide each topic into studies; each study into lessons; each lesson into specific facts and formulae. Let the child proceed step-by-step to master each one of these separate parts. . . . Subject-matter furnishes the end, and it determines the method. The child is simply the immature being who is to be matured; he is the superficial being who is to be deepened. . . . It is his to receive, to accept. His part is fulfilled when he is ductile and docile. (pp. 12–13)

The Essentialist philosophy thrives on a content-centered worldview. The child is a mere visitor in the adult world. Essentialism treats childhood as a useless point from which to depart as soon as possible through the use of prepackaged and static content arranged from an adult perspective. Childhood is viewed as a speed bump on the way to adulthood that needs to be dispensed with quickly so the mature job of collecting, storing, and regurgitating facts can begin in earnest. Students must learn science like scientists, or practice math like mathematicians. Unfortunately, children are not mini-adults, and they don't learn well when prepackaged curricular programs treat them that way.

The Essentialist curricular focus on preparation for the world as it is today also implies that the current knowledge base, social class structure, the state of democracy, laws, morals and mores are good enough and do not need to evolve or improve. The egalitarian spirit is not a concern of the Essentialist philosophy. An emphasis on a predetermined collection of knowledge ignores the need to question the current state of societal affairs or think critically about one's place in the world. Complex, creative, or innovative thinking is not valued because it does not fit within the predetermined content and expected answers. The logic behind the Essentialist philosophy is that if nothing needs to change, then there is no need create, innovate, evolve, diversify, expand or extend knowledge. There is only the need for the regurgitation, reproduction, and efficient demonstration of a standardized set of knowledge. Therefore, low-level imitative thinking is valued in an Essentialist curricular program.

There is a devotion to the fatally flawed belief in mental discipline by followers of the Essentialist philosophy. Mental Discipline is the belief that the brain can be exercised through experiences with subject matter that is considered difficult, in order to build a cognitive storehouse of knowledge (Thorndike, 1924). Essentialists believe that curriculum is supposed to be difficult and only the mentally strong will survive and progress to higher levels of education: Essentialists champion the slogan *no pain, no gain.*

Student effort and struggle is valued over interest and experience; "Grit" is often cited by Essentialists as an important disposition for students to possess. Certain academic subjects are valued because they are supposedly better for the mind or develop personal grit. Thorndike (1924) destroyed the mental discipline house of anti-intellectual cards years ago when his landmark studies found that students used more of their knowledge and transferred more of it to the real world in classes like wood shop and industrial arts as compared to classes traditionally recognized as "hard" and "rigorous" like Latin or algebra.

Mental discipline assumes standardization of curricula and instructional methods because there can be only one path to academic greatness: the difficult path. Researchers from the landmark Eight-Year Study explained that under the theory of mental discipline (Giles, McCutchen, and Zechiel, 1942) "all individuals were presumed to have minds possessing identical faculties that needed training. Education was carried on with little or no regard for the interests or needs of the learner" (p. 3).

> The ultimate act of transferring knowledge to daily use through experience does not occur in learning environments dominated by the mental discipline espoused by Essentialists. Although the rhetoric relies on slogans such as rigorous content and deep learning, Essentialist programs are surprisingly shallow repositories of knowledge disconnected from each other and the realities of integrated daily use of knowledge and skills and child development. The programs rely on mechanistic methods aimed at efficient and cost effective knowledge imitation and regurgitation, not creation and innovation.

Curricula modeled on ideas from mental discipline do not provide opportunities for connections and transfers between content and student experiences because student experiences and knowledge transfer are not valued in the Essentialist philosophy. The goal is to accumulate knowledge and regurgitate it in traditional forms such as recitations and commercially prepared standardized tests.

Extreme Behaviorism

Essentialist programs accomplish their aims of knowledge accumulation and regurgitation via the primitive idea that people will act rationally when confronted with a narrow set of choices. Proponents of standardization believe that teachers, students, and parents will conform to a standardized view of education. They mandate specific forms of teaching and learning that are enforced with rewards and punishments. The narrow view of teaching and learning represents an extreme strain of behaviorist theory.

One major weakness of policies harvested from extreme behaviorist theories is that they do not have a demonstrated record of success. That is because the strain of behaviorism used in many standardization programs rests upon the idea of control. Stimulus–Response psychology is at the heart of behaviorist policies that support standardization. Stimulus–Response psychology is the "science for controlling others" (Bredo, 2002, p. 25).

Think Pavlov's dog and you will be close to the idea held by some proponents of standardization that the use of punishment and lack of punishment will achieve the desired education goals (Rescorla and Wagner, 1972). Race to the Top grant requirements, No Child Left Behind (NCLB) waiver components, teacher evaluation schemes in approximately forty states, and commercially prepared standardized high school exit exams all rely on basic Stimulus–Response psychologically to achieve their goals. In essence, the bureaucrats in those states treat their education systems and those who work and learn in them like Pavlov's dog (Rescorla and Wagner, 1972).

Dewey described the situation of top-down education imposition and control when he explained the differences between the old and new education (1938/1997):

> The traditional scheme is, in essence, one of imposition from above and from outside. It imposes adult standards, subject-matter, and methods upon those who are only growing slowly toward maturity. The gap is so great that the required subject-matter, the methods of learning and of behaving are foreign to the existing capacities of the young. They are beyond the reach of the experience the young learner already possesses. Consequently, they must be imposed; even though good teachers will use devices of art to cover up the imposition so as to relieve it of obviously brutal features. (p. 19)

Policies created from theories and science based on controlling others with rewards and punishments have no place in a democratic public school system based on egalitarian principles or a public school system in which complex thinking, creativity, and innovation are said to be high priorities, as they are by the purveyors of the PISA, TIMSS, Common Core (National Governors Association and Council of Chief State School Officers [NGA & CCSSO], 2015), and proponents of standardization more generally. Policies based on extreme behaviorism create a narrowing of curriculum and teaching due to their reliance on fear as a motivation tool.

Teachers, students, parents, and school leaders are afraid to deviate from the edicts and compliance mandates of education bureaucrats for fear of some form of punishment (Au, 2011). Stimulus–Response policies do not lead to more innovative or creative thinking and teaching, nor do they foster higher levels of strategizing, and problem solving. They lead to curricular retrenchment, students becoming passive receptacles of information, and teachers becoming scared to try new things (Au, 2011; Dewey, 1938/1997; Freire 2000).

The reader should not take this section as an indictment on all of the research on behaviorism. The results from over 100 years of research have helped build a better understanding of how humans learn, react, and interact with content knowledge and their environment. The issue taken is the primitive application of the most extreme strains of behaviorism that, at their inception, were not intended to be applied to public education but instead were meant to understand better the differences between man and animal (Watson, 1913).

The results and findings derived from behaviorism have been refined over the years to inform pedagogy and andragogy, but proponents of standardization programs based on Stimulus–Response theory choose to use the most primitive of behaviorist aspects. It is a contradiction that pits the attributes necessary for maintaining a democracy in an uncertain future of global competitiveness against a policy quest to cement the past. Dewey (1938/1997) described the Stimulus–Response standardization contradiction as the "cultural product of societies that assumed the future would be much like the past, and yet it is used as educational food in a society where change is the rule, not the exception" (p. 19).

Proponents of standardization are essentially destroying the future to return to what they believe was a less complex and more academically rigorous past. They are trying to limit the complexity of the future through simplistic plans and policies based on flawed theories and philosophies.

Linguistic Relativism

Why, if there is at least 100 years of empirical research that documents the limitations of standardization in terms of providing all children in a democracy the opportunities necessary to reach high levels of education and develop better their capacities for complex thinking, can the latest crop of proponents of standardization state otherwise? Relativism plays a role in the marketing rhetoric that supports the Essentialist philosophy and the suppression of the truth about the limiting effects of standardization. It is the invisible backdrop in the ongoing fairy tale known as *creativity can be standardized.*

Relativism includes a set of beliefs that supports the position that all truths are local (Baghramian, 2004). Think of the saying "it's all relative" and you come close to the belief system. Facts only matter if they matter "here" so to speak. That type of relativist belief system allows proponents to dispense with or ignore the results of science if those results do not matter "here" or if they go against the standardized belief system. Relativism allows one to accept the idea that there exists no absolute truths. It is an anti-intellectual free-for-all.

All the so-called facts are open for interpretation and acceptance or rejection: Truth and meaning come from the individual's worldview. Therefore, if the individual believes that standardization will lead to greater acquisition of the attributes necessary to ensure public school students are globally competitive, then it must be true. The failure of standardization to produce the results that proponents claim should be produced are not caused by faulty suppositions and the junk-science underlying standardization. Failure to achieve the educational bounty promised by proponents of standardization is blamed on external factors like teachers, students, and parents.

Relativism is the ultimate insurance policy for proponents of standardization to never have to say they are sorry or wrong. The proponents do not have to acknowledge the failures of standardization because it is not true to them. The proponents need only believe that the public school system, and those within it, are the causes of failure, and the proponents need to only claim it publically to be true. Since the system has been declared broken then it must be broken. Evidence derived from science is not necessary (Lyotard, 1984). If the proponent happens to be the lead education policy maker in the country or state, then federal and/or state education policy might also reflect the proponent's worldview because the policy maker declares it so.

When proponents of standardization make public declarations like "a common set of student expectations for the entire United States is necessary for global competitiveness" they engage in linguistic relativism (Niemeier and Dirvin, 2000). Some proponents of standardization know that language influences thoughts and they know from history that if they say something enough times, for a long enough period of time, they have a chance that a growing number of people will think it is true. Consider widespread acceptance of the claim that public schools are failing and that the entire system needs to be reformed. Years of linguistic relativist rhetoric made the false claim an accepted truth.

Although the data suggest otherwise, the mantra that the public school system is failing to prepare students for the globally competitive economic future has successfully been used to push standardization proposals across the United States. The acceptance of the need to standardize on a large scale was not achieved because of scientific research, but more from the coordinated use of linguistic relativism and junk science. In essence, the sun can revolve around the Earth once again because enough people believe that it does. Not because results from science have confirmed it, but because linguistic relativists have said it for a long enough time and describe it in ways that make it sound like common sense. Science be damned.

Lyotard (1984) discussed the creative use of language to make the absurd seem logical as *language games* (p. 10). Lyotard presented the analogy of the use of language to influence others as a chess game. Every word within every statement is chosen carefully. Consider the terms "rigorous content" or "academic excellence" or "globally competitive" as examples. It is difficult for one to argue against those terms without seeming like one expects less of students or does not value excellence, outstanding education for all students, or global competitiveness. Their linguistic facades hide policies built on broken theories and junk science.

Cult of Specificity

Policy initiatives that result in the standardization of knowledge at the K–12 levels of education, in particular, the use of grade-level state-mandated, performance output curriculum standards, that flow from the traditionalist view of education, born out of Essentialist philosophical streams. The philosophical streams are buttressed by extreme behaviorism and linguistic relativism and they coalesce into what Tanner and Tanner (2007, p. 120) termed the *Cult of Specificity*.

Rigid, one-size-fits-all curriculum standards built on Essentialist conceptions have the expected outputs and the format of the outputs of the intended curriculum specified in detail. In turn, the expected outputs and their accepted forms dictate overtly the methods of instruction that violate the nature of the learner as an active constructor of meaning who brings prior experience and knowledge to the learning situation and the nature of knowledge as a fusion of subject matter and student experiences (Dewey, 1902). There is a cultlike belief that greater specificity leads to higher levels of student output and less variance in student output.

Take, for example, the Common Core Grade 7 Literacy Standard, RL.7.6: "Determine an author's point of view or purpose in a text and analyze how the author distinguishes his or her position from that of others" (NGA and CCSSO, 2010). The verbs "determine" and "analyze" specify the expected output actions to be demonstrated by the student in order to demonstrate mastery of the standard. In this example, actions that require more complex creative or strategic thinking such as critique, evaluate, create, or reimagine would not be acceptable demonstrations of mastery. For instance, CCSS for high school include very few standards, less than 11 percent in math, and less than 30 percent in language arts that foster creative or strategic thinking (Sforza, Tienken, and Kim, 2016).

The grade-by-grade specificity of the CCSS, coupled with the standardized testing of the Core, creates de *facto* pacing expectations for student mastery and the pace of teaching. The CCSS were designed as mastery standards. Students are expected to demonstrate mastery of every standard at every grade level on the specified dates of the tests or by the end of the school year.

Cognitive, social, and emotional developmental differences of children are not factored into the construction of the standards or standardization programs in general. In addition, there are not standards in each grade level that represent "above" or "below" grade-level expectations, making it difficult to meet the needs of students whose readiness levels are far below or above the expected standards. The specificity of the standards acts as an academic cattle chute that forces conformity upon the entire system in terms of curriculum, instruction, and assessment.

Further, the CCSS include appendices in which specific examples of language arts texts, mathematical representations, and student outcomes are presented to further define what is considered acceptable student demonstration of mastery. Hence, educators feel pressured to use the specific materials listed in the CCSS to accomplish the specific standards and thus create a de facto type of specified instruction that students experience throughout their education careers. In effect, the specific nature of products like the CCSS and the products it recommends for use set up an assembly line of education that specifies the output in the form of standardized expectations and testing from kindergarten to high school graduation. In turn, the methods of teaching and the materials used also become highly specified.

The implied message of the standardized curricula products and their corresponding examples is that there exist specific student and teacher behaviors and demonstrations that represent achievement of the standards. The implied message of specification has the covert effect of reducing teaching to imitation or following recipes or sets of rules, or technical manuals to achieve a standardized outcome in the specific format and level of imitated difficulty. Dewey (1929) noted an insidious influence of standardized specificity on teaching when he wrote:

> In this situation there is a strong tendency to identify teaching ability with the use of procedures that yield immediately successful results, success being measured by such things as order in the classroom, correct recitations by pupils in assigned lessons, passing of examinations, promotion of pupils to a higher grade, etc. (p. 15)

Thus, as Dewey stated, not only is the content tightly specified, the corresponding teaching methods tend to become mechanical and based more on "how to do things", and over time, teachers learn to imitate the examples and content found in the standards and they begin to "want recipes" (Dewey, 1929, pp. 15–16) for prepackaged standardized outcomes. Standardization deskills teachers to the levels of drones and followers instead of leaders and creators of learning.

Giles, McCutchen, and Zechiel (1942) described similar characteristics from the early 1900s that are unfortunately similar to standardization practices embedded in the Every Student Succeeds Act of 2015 in the post-NCLB era:

> At one time it was a question to be answered only by national commissions made up of research scholars known for their mastery of specific content fields. Then, state courses of study were formulated in the same pious hope that

> uniformity would produce excellence. The classroom teachers, barred from such profound considerations, meekly took the textbook handed them and marked off the doses by which the text was to be sequentially absorbed. (pp. 76–77)

One might substitute the words "computer" or "online content" for the word "textbooks" in the quote above, but the essences of the distally developed goals and specific objectives is the same. The professional educators are reduced to the role of an assembler of a product in a factory. The program outcomes are predetermined and all students receive more or less the same program aimed at the same outcomes. The standardization programs of the early 1900s failed miserably in terms of educating large percentages of the population. Consider that less than approximately 10 percent of students attended college in 1918 according to the Commission on the Reorganization of Secondary Education (1918) and little more than that by around 1930 (Aikin, 1942). Less students gaining less access and less education is one tragic result of the Cult of Specificity.

THEORY OF PERFORMATIVITY

The theory of performativity pervades all aspects of standardization. Lyotard (1984) explained that the theory of performativity revolves around the ability of a social system, in this case the public school system, to achieve the external goals set for it in the most efficient manner. Think, maximize output with minimal input and you are close to understanding the overall idea. Likewise, scientific management and the efficiency movement as propagated by Frederick Taylor (1947) includes the mindset found in performativity in terms of reliance of mass quantification of outputs based on narrow sets of goals and strict control of inputs and standardized processes.

The ultimate goal of the system according to the theory of performativity should be efficiency of the desired standardized outputs, not quality, creativity, or innovation. Policy makers who knowingly or unknowingly subscribe to the theory of performativity do not value inputs, processes, outputs, and monitoring schemes that are not efficient or that cannot be easily quantified and or measured. The publication of *A Nation at Risk* (National Commission on Excellence in Education [NCEE], 1983) ushered in Performativity 2.0 to the U.S. education policy arena following Frederick Taylor falling out of favor in policy-making circles. Eisner (1985) noted at the time that U.S. education policy focused on the achievement of prescribed and prespecified outputs. The narrow focus on outcomes creates a situation in which the curriculum is more of a product instead of a process. The curriculum becomes an end, as opposed to a means of achieving diverse ends. Once curriculum becomes a product instead of a professional process, it is open to standardization and the negative effects of performativity.

The performativity rhetoric surrounding the need to standardize expectations resonates with calls for higher levels of performance on standardized assessments such as PISA, PARCC, SBAC, or the latest state tests sold by the proponents of standardization. In turn, the monitoring devices such as standardized tests measure only those skills easy to measure, in formats that are highly efficient to score and report, like on a personal computing device. The administration of the tests is tightly monitored, as are the results.

State education agencies report the results from the standardized tests in language that reflects the linguistic relativism, an Essentialist philosophical worldview, and theory of performativity. For example, the widely used term "college and career ready" creates an imaginary line of demarcation between groups of students. The term insinuates that one is simultaneously college and career ready, or not, and that the results from one standardized test can provide that determination. It further creates the impression that there is a standardized path one can follow to achieve college and career readiness. Never mind that there are over 4,400 colleges and universities in the United States with their own diverse criteria and expectations, and tens-of-thousands of careers, requiring vastly different sets of skills, content, and dispositions.

The term "college and career ready" is simply another prefabricated layer of performativity expectations and monitoring placed upon a system to cement standardization. How could all students be college and career ready at the same time? Nowhere on the planet are all students college ready, let alone gainfully employed in their career of choice upon graduating high school. The term college and career ready has no grounding in empirical evidence but it creates a convenient, easily monitored data point within a system based on performativity.

The layers of specifying and monitoring performance create artificial limits on the number of educators, schools, and school districts that can be categorized as effectively meeting the standardized performance targets because the targets are arbitrary and unrealistic. Policies based on the theory of performativity ensure that most of the system is in a constant state of failure in order to maintain high levels of uncertainty and pressure for more performance; enough is never enough.

Take for example the ranking of schools based on student standardized test performance that is an important component of the performativity systems in fifty states. Schools that show growth in standardized test results can still be sanctioned if their total results sufficiently lag the schools in their predetermined peer group of schools. For example, schools that manage to demonstrate growth on standardized test results and meet or exceed their peer group aggregate results can still be sanctioned if they do not meet or exceed the state averages for aggregate performance. Schools that demonstrate growth, exceed their peer groups, and exceed state averages for aggregate performance can still be sanctioned if one of the many student subgroups, such as special education, underperforms a state-mandated target in some way.

There are myriad ways for the system of performance monitoring to judge and snare a school and keep it and its educators and students in a state of constant monitoring and uncertainty. It is the state of uncertainty that helps drive conformity within the theory of performativity. Ball (2010) described the apparatus used to actualize the theory of performativity and the constant state of uncertainty for those educators assaulted by the policies based on performativity:

> It is the data-base, the appraisal meeting, the annual review, report writing, the regular publication of results and promotion applications, inspections and peer reviews that are mechanics of performativity. The teacher, researcher, academic are subject to a myriad of judgments, measures, comparisons and targets. Information is collected continuously, recorded and published. . . . Within all this, there is a high degree of uncertainty and instability. A sense of being constantly judged in different ways, by different means, according to different criteria, through different agents and agencies. There is a flow of changing demands, expectations and indicators that makes one continually accountable and constantly recorded . . . unsure whether we are doing enough, doing the right thing, doing as much as others, or as well as others, constantly looking to improve, to be better, to be excellent. And yet it is not always very clear what is expected. (p. 220)

Ball described accurately the current state of teacher and school administrator evaluation policies and programs. There is constant monitoring of performance through several means and final evaluation of performance can result in corrective action, loss of tenure, or dismissal in some states. The stakes are very high for teachers and school administrators. In some cases the multiple sets of expectations conflict in their aims and means.

Take for example some of the classroom teacher evaluation criteria currently used in many states. Some of the criteria require teachers to empower students in the classroom and teach them how to learn, not only what to learn. The criteria require the teachers create opportunities for active learning, divergent thinking, student decision-making, and creativity. These types of criteria go a long way to help make a classroom student-centered, yet they run headlong into standardized curriculum expectations like those found in the CCSS and expectations of performance on standardized tests that require convergent thinking and passive learning (Sforza, Tienken, and Kim, 2016).

Teachers and school administrators who worry about their employment based on results from standardized tests tend to narrow their leadership and instruction because they feel pressured to make sure all the content is covered for the test (Au, 2011). Covering the content places students in the mode of passive receptacle of information and violates the teaching criteria necessary to receive the highest marks for their evaluation scores. School administrators pressure teachers and teachers work students toward finding the expected correct answer most likely to appear on the high-stakes standardized test rather than teaching them how to learn and how to think divergently and creatively.

Thus, teachers are caught between choosing the best bad option. Like Odysseus deciding whether to battle Scylla or Charybdis as he navigated the strait of Messina during his epic voyage, teachers feel they are left with no good choice (Fagles, 1997). Either choice has negative consequences. Like Odysseus before them, teachers must take the best worst option in their estimation. They must make the choice between methods they think will result in covering more content in preparation for a standardized test or methods that will result in better learning for students but end up penalizing the teacher on his or her test scores and lead to punishment because they fear they will not cover as much content.

As teachers improve on one set of expectations, like test scores through the use of standardized teaching methods aligned to the test, they are potentially causing themselves to appear less effective on another set of expectations, classroom observations of teaching. As Ball (2010) described, teachers are snared in the net of performativity. Each avenue of action leads eventually to a failing grade on one of the many aspects of their performance evaluation.

The policies of standardization and monitoring are having the intended effect on teachers of creating uncertainty and pressure. Anderson (2005) described some of the effects of policies based on the theory of performativity at the outset of NCLB as increases in early retirement, more workplace stress and stress-related illness for teachers, and more emotional stress for students because of the high stakes testing mandates.

The effects described by Anderson (2005) also have the consequence of cleansing the system of people who might challenge or resist the policies of performativity. Over time, the system becomes populated with people who identify with, acquiesce to, or overtly support policies of performativity. Although perhaps well intentioned, the unknowing or unquestioning followers of performativity contribute to the overall degradation of the democratic tradition and egalitarian spirit of the public school system and become an aid to the slow transformation toward standardization and conformity. They do not question the system. They simply become part of it and complicit in the weakening and destruction of public school and hence, the long-term health of democracy and students' future opportunities.

Opportunity Costs

The costs of standardization are high, and not just in dollars and cents. What are students not receiving or experiencing when they are forced to comply with a system of standardization based on performativity? How are teachers deskilled in a system of intense monitoring, and stripped of their professionalism in the name of efficiency? What other experiences could teachers provide students with the time they use to prepare them for standardized tasks? How many student passions and future interests are being destroyed in order to return the U.S. public school system to the mechanized past?

It is easier to tally the monetary costs to a school system to implement standardized programs. It is more difficult to judge the long-term cost to some students who, at an early age, realize they don't fit into the standardized system. Stress, disinterest, low self-efficacy, sadness, boredom, and frustration are some of the costs not recognized by those mandating policies of performativity (Suldo, Shaunessy, Thalji, Michalowski, and Shaffer, 2009). Proponents of performativity view the negative consequences of standardization as being due to personal weakness, lack of grit, the wrong mind-set and inefficiencies by those administering the system of standardization. Democracy, childhood, diversity, interests and passions, creativity, and human development in general are not valued because they are not efficient.

OUT OF THE SHADOWS

Plato's *Republic* and his allegory of "The Cave" (Plato, *Republic*. 514a–515c. Translated by Kamtekar, 2003) is a helpful example to understand, how in the face of so much evidence to the contrary, proponents of standardization continue to vend the false promises of broken theories and philosophies to the American public. In the allegory of "The Cave," Plato describes Socrates working with his student Glaucon. Socrates explains the situation of the cave to help Glaucon understand that sometimes people feel safe within the clasps of mental chains that bind their minds to simplistic explanations and false fears masked at the truth:

> Imagine an underground chamber like a cave, with a long entrance open to the daylight and as wide as the cave. In this chamber are men who have been prisoners there since they were children, their legs and necks being so fastened that they can only look straight ahead and cannot turn their heads. Some way off, behind and higher up, a fire is burning, and between the fire and the prisoners and above them runs a road, in front of which a curtain-wall has been built, like the screen at puppet shows between the operators and their audience, above

> which they show their puppets. . . . For, tell me, do you think our prisoners could see anything of themselves or their fellows except the shadows thrown by the fire on the wall of the cave opposite them? Would they not assume the shadows they saw were real things? Glaucon replied, "Inevitably."

According to Plato, Socrates continued:

> And so in every way they would believe that the shadows of the objects we mentioned were the whole truth. Glaucon replied, "Yes, inevitably." (Plato, *Republic*. 514a–515c. Translated by Kamtekar, 2003)

Proponents of standardization have a problem. They unquestionably cling to the outdated and anti-intellectual ideological chains that bind them to positions built on falsehoods based on worn out slogans and dogma. They are in an echo chamber of junk science and linguistic relativism; a self-imposed cave of the curricular surreal. Proponents of standardization are using ideas from the 1800s that have been scientifically disproved, and proclaiming them as the remedies for problems of the modern world.

Standardization relies on mass-production techniques, left over from the industrial revolution, as principles for the delivery of public education. Proponents isolate themselves with elitist national committees, state commissions, and Blue-Ribbon panels that in some cases either knowingly choose to shun the findings of science or are unaware of scientific findings. They then masquerade as democratic participants with public hearings, but seldom act on evidence or requests from the public.

Rugg described a similar scene of reform from the 1920s. It was almost identical to that of the development and implementation of the Common Core in 2010 (1927):

> In 1890, mass-education, like its compatriot, economic mass production, was ready for standardization, crystallization. . . . For nearly a century as we have seen, professional textmakers and professors of subjects prepared textbooks and the textbook dominated the curriculum. (pp. 33, 35–36)

Substitute the word "standards" for "textbook" and you have the current reform mentality that drove products like the Common Core and the national testing programs. But Rugg was not describing the Common Core, he was critiquing the work the Committee of Ten from 1893 and the prior 100 years of curriculum making in the United States that was dominated by ideas of curricular standardization based on expected outputs.

Rugg derided the overwhelming influence of college presidents who wanted standardized student output from which to make college entrance decisions more standardized, efficient, and hence less costly to their institutions. Rugg described the college entrance requirements as a driving force of standardization and opposed to democratic diversity (1927):

> To students of politics and culture, freedom from standardization is a positive indication of the worth of democracy, but to college presidents and principals of private preparatory schools, it was anathema. Diversity in school curricula produced difficulty of administration; hence it was not to be tolerated. (p. 36)

The current reform movement incorporates college entrance requirements into the reform rhetoric through the use of ambiguous slogans such as "college and career ready" and "globally competitive." College entrance is now, in the post-NCLB era, an expected output of public school curriculum design as evidenced by students as young as kindergarten being labeled college and career ready in some states.

Rugg's comments appear almost prophetic in terms of how the Essentialist calls for college and career ready academic performance and global competitiveness have been the driving force for standardization, yet the rhetoric sounds student centered, such as in the name for the 2015 renewal of the Elementary and Secondary Education Act, known as the Every Student Succeeds Act. There is a lot of general talk about individual students in the act but the policies and practices that result from the talk is decidedly standardized and driven by distal forces. Rugg (1927) critiqued the forked-tongue messages of the proponents of standardization from the late 1800s that seems eerily similar to the messages being sent by some policy makers and bureaucrats today:

> Although giving lip service to the creed that the high school is the "people's college," both college presidents and headmasters of the private school (and it must also be said of a considerable body of high-school principals) wanted the high-school curriculum standardized on the basis of preparation for the higher institutions. And they had their way. For twenty years college presidents and preparatory-school people took charge, determining the form and spirit of the materials of instruction throughout the entire range of the school. (p. 36)

To change their positions means proponents of standardization must admit failure of their beliefs and in some cases their actions and their lucrative products. It is easier to believe in the messages hidden in the shadows of the reform cave rather than accept the evidence and the responsibility.

EXITING THE CAVE

The words of Coniglione (2015) provide simple guidance to those who seek to exit the ideological cave of standardization: "Stay aware of the need to know *what* to watch and *how* to see, not merely operate unconsciously" (p. 21). Science matters and just because someone claims that standardization of education expectations and curriculum output produces superior results does not make it true. Public school educators must come out of the shadows and break the chains of standardization. They must watch the policies and practices carefully so they can see the encroachment of standardization and performativity on their own thinking and actions and ultimately on the lives of the children whom they are intrusted.

The constricting influence of the specificity of standardization built on a philosophy of Essentialism and the theory of performativity becomes an antagonist to creativity, innovation, and strategic thinking, especially if those ways of thinking are not specified in the expected curriculum standards. The confluence of regressive theories and philosophies create what Kliebard (1999) called Spartan education, harkening back to the ancient Greek city-state of Sparta in which efficiency and extreme regimentation were valued.

Kliebard (1999) used the term Spartan to describe the basic conception of standardized education driven by facts and social Darwinian grit. But then again, how can one specify and mandate creativity or innovation in a way that allows for true creativity and innovation? Creativity cannot be standardized.

In effect, too much specificity and standardization retards creative and strategic thinking if great care is not taken to overtly include multiple opportunities within any curriculum standards for teachers to teach creatively and students to have consistent practice exploring and using creative and strategic thinking (Sternberg, 2003). There must be flexible, locally developed standards that are more like ideas that can be customized, and less like mandates. The way out of the standardization cave can be found by following a curriculum paradigm based on diversifying education around skills and dispositions that transcend content and time. Curriculum must allow for multiple pathways for learning and demonstration of learning based on developmentally pliable aims.

NEXT STEPS

The issue is not whether there should be standards for curriculum and assessment. There have always been curriculum standards in every public school. They used to be locally called the board of education approved school curriculum. Local standards, developed at cognitively, socially, and morally flexible levels of mastery, and informed from many sources, but not mandated, should form the basis for a comprehensive local curriculum customized for the students who are compelled to experience it.

One must look beyond the boundaries of the United States in search of skills that will help students to remain not only the most economically competitive, but also culturally literate and democratic participants in a global community. There is a need to go beyond the nineteenth-century mindset being used in U.S. education policy making based on monitoring, compliance, conformity, and convergence. It is improbable that Americans will compete for routine manufacturing jobs that pay $10 a day in China or $2 in Bangladesh (China Labour Bulletin, 2013). Yet that is the mindset that drives standardization and current U.S. education reform.

There will always be workers from other developing countries to fill the routine jobs when China and Bangladesh price themselves out of the market. Some Southeast Asian countries like Vietnam and some African countries such as Nigeria are poised to step in. The world that gave birth to the ideologies, theories, and philosophies that support standardization no longer exists, and it is not coming back. Accumulation and imitation of knowledge will not drive an innovation economy yet that is what standardized curriculum expectations value. The proponents of standardization are unknowingly destroying the future to return to the past by choosing to cling to outdated thinking.

Science and artistry must be used in the development of curricula that foster creativity and innovation in ways that respect the unique passions and interests of students and educators while maintaining an eye on the future in ways that are democratic and egalitarian. There will forever be countries in which people with routine knowledge and skills will work for substantially less money and live in conditions that many in the United States would find appalling.

Racing to the standardized curricular bottom to compete with countries poised to perform routine jobs for five dollars a day is not a viable solution to global competitiveness in the knowledge. The knowledge economy runs on creativity, innovation, socially conscious problem solving, entrepreneurship and other unstandardized skills and dispositions that the United States population possess in large amounts due in part to our previously unstandardized school system.

In part II of the book, the last three chapters, some guiding principles found in the classical and contemporary literature are provided to keep in mind when developing policies and programs for curriculum, instruction, and assessment in public schools. An existing progressive-experimentalist paradigm is presented that educators can use to guide them as they proceed to unstandardized and diversify curriculum and instruction. An example set of unstandardized skills and dispositions are presented as well as specific examples educators can use to design, develop, evolve, and implement their own versions of evidence-based, customized, unstandardized curricula.

REFERENCES

Aikin, W.M. (1942). *The story of the eight-year study*. New York: Harper.

Anderson, G.L. (2005). Performing school reform in the age of political spectacle. In Alexander, Anderson, & Gallegos (Eds.), *Performance theories in education: Power, pedagogy, and the politics of identity*, 199–220.

Atkinson, A.B., & Leigh, A. (2008). Top income in New Zealand 1921–2005: Understanding the effects of marginal tax rates, migration threat, and the macroeconomy. *Review of Income and Wealth, 54*(2), 149–165.

Au, W. (2011) Teaching under the new Taylorism: high-stakes testing and the standardization of the 21st century curriculum. *Journal of Curriculum Studies, 43*(1), 25–45. DOI: 10.1080/00220272.2010.521261.

Baghramian, M. (2004). *Relativism*. London: Routledge.

Ball, S.J. (2010). The teacher's soul and the terrors of performativity. *Journal of Education Policy, 18*(2), 215–228. Retrieved from http://dx.doi.org/10.1080/0268093022000043065.

Bannister, R. (1989). *Social Darwinism: Science and myth in Anglo-American social thought*. Philadelphia: Temple University Press.

Bon Jovi, J., Bryan, D., & Sambora, R. (1992). In these arms. On *keep the faith* [CD]. Nashville: Mercury Records.

Bredo, E. (2002). The Darwinian center to the vision of William James. In J. Garrison, P. Poedeschi, & E. Bredo (Eds.), *William James and education*. New York: Teachers College Press.

China Labour Bulletin. (2013). *Wages and employment*. Author. Retrieved from http://www.clb.org.hk/en/view-resource-centre-content/100206.

Commission on the Reorganization of Secondary Education. (1918). *Cardinal principles of secondary education*. Washington, DC: U.S. Bureau of Education, Bulletin No. 35.

Coniglione, F. (2015) "Introduzione. Complessità del reale, semplicità del pensiero" In I. Licata, (Ed.), *I gatti di Wiener. Riflessioni sistemiche sulla complessità*. Bonanno Editore, Acireale-Roma 2015, p. 21.

Dewey, J. (1938/1997). *Experience and education*. New York: Touchstone.

Dewey, J. (1929). *Sources of science in education*. New York: Liveright.

Dewey, J. (1916). *Democracy and education*. New York: McMillan.

Dewey, J. (1915). *School and society*. Chicago, IL: University of Chicago Press.

Dewey, J. (1902). *The child and the curriculum*. Chicago, IL: The University of Chicago Press.

Eisner, E. (1985). Learning and teaching the ways of knowing. In K. Rehage & E. Eisner (Eds.), *Eighty-fourth yearbook of the National Society for the study of education, Part 2*. Chicago, IL: University of Chicago Press.

Fagles, R. (1997). *The odyssey*. London: Penguin Books.

Frankenberg, E. (2011). Educational charter schools: A civil rights mirage? *Kappa Delta Pi Record, 47*(3), 100–105.

Freire, P. (2000). *Pedagogy of the oppressed: 30th anniversary edition*. New York: Continuum.

Giles, H.H., McCutchen, S.P., & Zechiel, A.N. (1942). *Adventures in American education volume II: Exploring the curriculum*. New York: Harper and Brothers.

Hungerford, T.L. (2012). *Taxes and the economy: An economic analysis of the top tax rates since 1945*. Congressional Research Service. Retrieved from http://graphics8.nytimes.com/news/business/0915taxesandeconomy.pdf.

Kamtekar, R. (2003). *Plato: The Republic*. London: Penguin Books.

Kliebard, H. (1999). The liberal arts curriculum and its enemies: The effort to redefine general education. In K.J. Rehage (Ed.), *Issues in curriculum: A selection of chapters from past NSSE yearbooks*. Chicago, IL: University of Chicago Press.

Lyotard, J.F. (1984). The postmodern condition: A report on knowledge. *Theory and history of literature, Volume 10*. Manchester, UK: Manchester University Press.

Miron, G., Urschel, J.L., Mathis, W.J., & Tornquist, E. (2010). *Schools without diversity: Education management organizations, charter schools and the demographic stratification of the American school system*. Tempe: Education and the Public Interest Center & Education Policy Research Unit. Retrieved from http://epicpolicy.org/publication/schools-without-diversity.

National Commission on Excellence in Education [NCEE]. (1983). *A nation at risk*. Washington, DC: U.S. Department of Education.

National Governors Association and Council of Chief State School Officers [NGA & CCSSO]. (2015). *Common Core state standards: English Language arts*. Washington, DC: NGA and CCSSO. Retrieved from http://www.corestandards.org/about-the-standards/frequently-asked-questions/#faq-2309.

Niemeier, S. & Dirven, R. (Eds). (2000). *Evidence for linguistic relativity*. Amsterdam: John Benjamins Publishing Company.

Rescorla, R.A. & Wagner, A.R. (1972). A theory of Pavlovian conditioning: Variations in the effectiveness of reinforcement and nonreinforcement. In A.H. Black & W.F. Prokasy (Eds.), *Classical conditioning II: Current theory and research* (pp. 64–99). New York: Appleton-Century.

Roemer, J. (1998). *Equality of opportunity*. Cambridge: Harvard University Press.

Rugg, H. (1927). Three decades of mental discipline. Curriculum-making via national committees. In H. Rugg (Ed.), *Part I curriculum making past and present, The twenty-sixth yearbook of the national society for the study of education*. Bloomington, IN: Public School Publishing, 33–65.

Sforza, D., Tienken, C.H., & Kim, E. (2016). A comparison of higher-order thinking in the grades 9–12 Common Core State Standards and the 2009 New Jersey content standards for English language arts and mathematics. *AASA Journal of Scholarship and Practice*, *12*(4), 4–32.

Simon, K. & Grant, W.V. (1965). *Digest of Educational Statistics*, Office of Education, Bulletin 1965, No. 4. Washington, DC: U.S. Government Printing Office.

Sirin, S.R. (2005). Socioeconomic status and academic achievement: A meta-analytic review of research. *Review of Educational Research, 75*(3), 417–453.

Sternberg, R.J. (2003). Creative thinking in the classroom. *Scandinavian Journal of Educational Research*, *47*, 325–338.

Suldo, S.M., Shaunessy, E., Thalji, A., Michalowski, J., & Shaffer, E. (2009). Sources of stress for students in high school preparatory and general education programs:

Group differences and associations with adjustment. *Adolescence, 44*(176), 925–948.

Tanner, D. & Tanner, L. (2007). *Curriculum development: Theory into practice.* Upper Saddle River, NJ: Pearson.

Taylor, F.W. (1947). *Scientific management.* New York: Harper and Brothers.

Thorndike, E.L. (1924). Mental discipline in high school studies. *Journal of Educational Psychology, 15*, 1–22, 98.

Tienken, C.H. (2016). Standardized test results can be predicted, so stop using them to drive education policymaking. In C. Tienken & C. Mullen (Eds.), *Education policy perils: Tackling the tough issues* (pp. 157–185). Philadelphia, PA: Taylor Francis Routledge.

Tienken, C.H. (2013). Neoliberalism, social Darwinism, and consumerism masquerading as school reform. *Interchange, 43*, 295–316. DOI: 0.1007/s10780-013-9178-y.

Tienken, C.H. & Orlich, D.C. (2013). *The school reform landscape: Fraud, myth, and lies.* Lanham, MD: Rowman and Littlefield.

Tyler, R.W. (1949). *Basic principles of curriculum and instruction.* Chicago, IL: University of Chicago Press.

Watson, J.B. (1913). Psychology as the behaviorist views it. *Psychological Review, 20*, 158–178.

Part II

DEFYING STANDARDIZATION: TRANSLATING THEORY INTO PRACTICE

Chapter 5

Less Standardized for the Future

The United States and its territories comprise the third most populated country in the world with approximately 320 million people. Its borders encompass approximately 3.8 million square miles, or 9.8 million square kilometers, and span at least six time zones. The United States includes seven major geographic areas and 11 different climates. It is culturally diverse and more than 40 languages are spoken regularly. The United States is decidedly unstandardized and multifaceted in many ways.

Although the People's Republic of China and India have populations three to four times that of the United States, the U.S. population is larger than many of the core countries of the European Union combined (e.g., England, Germany, Italy, and France). The U.S. economy is the largest national economy in the world when measured by gross domestic product. The economies of many states in America are larger than those of other industrialized countries. For instance, if California were an independent nation it would have the world's 8th largest economy ahead of Russia, India, Italy, Canada, and Australia. The Texas economy would rank 14 in the world, ahead of South Korea, and New York would be 16, larger than the economies of Singapore, Argentina, and Norway.

What, So What, Now What

The obscene infatuation with having all public school students master, and demonstrate mastery, in the same format and with the same emphasis, of one set of static and finite content, or what I term the "What"-to-learn curriculum, is a dead end. A myopic focus on a narrow standardized curriculum based only on What-to-learn obfuscates student opportunities to engage in

"So What" and "Now What" complex, higher-order thinking. Standardization based on What-to-learn ultimately results in convergent thinking and less intellectual risk-taking on the part of educators and students. That is not to say that the *What*, or the traditional basic content knowledge, is not important. Traditional basic content knowledge such as mathematical computation or literal comprehension in reading are important when used as part of a larger, more diverse unstandardized view of curriculum that facilitates development of creative and complex thinking. Standardized, *What-to-learn* curricula can only ever be one leg of the three-legged curricular stool with creative and complex thinking forming a solid base for learning.

Carefully designed and less standardized curricula can foster higher-level thinking, referred to in this book as *So What* and *Now What* thinking. The So What of curriculum includes big-picture thinking, connecting the dots of content among concepts and experiences, and seeing the conceptual forest through the trees. Curricula designed to include So What content and activities provides students the opportunities to put all the "What" together to draw conclusions, make inferences, or to identify themes, morals, and patterns. So What opportunities allow students to grapple with, cogitate on, and synthesize thoughts about "What" *does it all mean?*

So What curricular experiences include activities in which students make connections among content areas, connections among content areas and themselves, and connections among content areas, themselves and the world outside of their world. The opportunities can be as complex as an entire course on the issues facing a democracy or as simple as prompts such as, "Explain what else this concept reminds you of from other subjects and your life."

Now What opportunities are purposeful experiences for students to connect the "What" to action. Curricula embedded with Now What experiences provide students opportunities to use what they learn in developmentally appropriate real-world, socially conscious situations. Experiences also allow for students to create new knowledge or redesign existing ideas to develop potential solutions to ill-structured, open-ended problems. Now What experiences provide students the opportunity to answer the questions like, "Now what can I do with this information or skill?" and "How can knowing this information or possessing this skill help others?" Curricula designed to develop Now What thinking is action oriented and provides diverse opportunities to engage in action-oriented experiences.

Given the economic, political, environmental, and socio-civic diversity and challenges faced by people living in the world's largest innovation economy in the twenty-first century, any discussion of curriculum design, development, and implementation needs to go beyond the skills needed in the industrial revolution age of the nineteenth century. A static one-size-fits-all set of curricular expectations will not suffice. There is no evidence that one set of curricular expectations produce superior academic results that correlate to any meaningful academic, economic, civic, or avocational measures.

Curricula designed, developed, and implemented in the twenty-first century must be diversified, pliable, less standardized, and connected to the unique needs and contexts of the students compelled to experience them. Curricula must attend to the multiple needs of economics, civics, and personal development. But what should be the content of such curricula?

FUNCTIONS OF PUBLIC EDUCATION

The question of curriculum content needs to be answered by the answer to another historic question: What are the purposes of public school? Goodlad (1983) borrowed from Dewey and others when he efficiently described the underpinnings of curriculum making:

> Rational process of curricular decision-making should be guided by a conception of why we have schools—of what schools are for. Schools should do what the rest of society does not do well and what individuals and society very much need. (p. 304).

Public school has historically had specific purposes centered around the fulfillment of three complementary functions: (1) *economic*: students experience a general set of knowledge and skills they can use as a platform to progress to specialized education for a vocation and economic independence; (2) *socio-civic*: knowledge and skills that help students gain experiences in being responsible and participating citizens in a democracy and the global community; and (3) *avocational*: knowledge, skills, and experiences that help students develop their personal interests, passions, and hobbies (Tanner and Tanner, 2007).

The authors of Volume II of the Eight-Year Study (Giles, McCutchen, and Zechiel, 1942) combined the three complementary functions of public school into two categories and described the purposes of public education to address the needs of the individual and society:

> In this definition of purpose, two broad guiding principles are evident: (1) the educational program should aid the learner in making effective adaptation to his environment in all its major aspects physical, economic, and social; (2) the educational program should develop in each individual those personal characteristics that will enable him to participate effectively in the preservation and extension of the culture. (p. 5)

Economic Function

The economic function of public school is the area that seems to receive the most attention from proponents of standardization policies and supporters of international testing. The economic function is the function targeted by standardization policies and practices aimed at increasing college and career readiness and the global competitiveness of students. The economic function of public schooling was a driving rhetorical force for standardization programs such as the Race to the Top grant program, the CCSS, and the national standardized testing programs SBAC and PARCC and the Every Student Succeeds Act.

Economic viability and standardization do not have to go hand in hand. One does not beget or need the other. As was argued in chapter 3, curricula expectations do not have to be standardized in order to achieve positive results in terms of the economic function of public school. The curricula should be (1) informed by evidence, (2) based on needs of students and the larger society, (3) unstandardized, and (4) multifaceted to achieve the various functions of a public school system in a democracy.

Socio-Civic Function

The socio-civic function of public education is one that seems to be overlooked by proponents of standardization. One historic role of public education has been that of the incubator of democracy in the United States. Public education has a history of uniting diverse peoples through exposure to a liberal education and providing the outlets for people to also specialize in diverse career-oriented areas (Commission on the Reorganization of Secondary Education, 1918; Dewey, 1899; 1916). It is the unifying and specializing characteristics of the United States public school system that provides a unique mixture of common yet diverse thinking and opportunities to follow one's interests and passions while still learning the democratic traditions of the United States so as to carry on and improve the republic for the common good (Aikin, 1942).

Dewey (1929) explained the socio-civic role of public education in nurturing a democracy:

> For the creation of a democratic society we need an educational system where the process of moral intellectual development is in practice as well as in theory a cooperative transaction of inquiry engaged in by free, independent human beings who treat ideas and the heritage of the past as means and methods for the further enrichment of life, quantitatively and qualitatively, who use the good attained for the discovery and establishment of something better. (p. 84).

How can students learn to actively participate in a democracy, critique political policy ideas, and think creatively, complexly, and innovatively if they are essentially educated in a system that is standardized, decidedly autocratic, and focused on convergent thinking? The autocratic nature of standardized programs is another contradiction of standardization.

Proponents claim standardization policies and programs will prepare students to be globally competitive and college and career ready, yet those same policies and programs do not address the underlying force that has driven the economic and overall global success of the United States: democracy. Proponents of standardization claim they want to produce critical thinkers yet their programs require conformity, imitation, and convergent thinking that does not critique or challenge the status quo or value divergent thinking.

Conant (1958) warned of the downsides of standardization through academic tracking via standardized curriculum policies. He used the example of the common European model of curriculum organization in which only a select percentage of students are exposed to the socio-civic aspect of liberal education in public schools. Those are the students who are then allowed to move on to the specializing function of education, but not until the college years. They are also the students who go on to occupy positions of power. The rest of the population is segregated out through standardized testing and relegated to a narrow curricula suited for lower-level job training and following the rules of the elites.

> The general education of the doctor, lawyer . . . or professional scholar is provided by special secondary schools, admission to which is determined by a highly selective procedure at age 10 or 11. Not more than 20 per cent of an age group selected from the elementary school are selected for preuniversity schools. Therefore there is a waste of talent under the European system. No one has estimated how much potential talent goes undeveloped in Germany, France, Italy, and Switzerland because of the early selection of preuniversity students, a selection often influenced by the class system of European lands. (p. 2).

Conant's (1958) comments ring true today. Only 12 percent of the population aged 25 to 64 in the European Union group of core 21 countries has attained at least a bachelor's degree (BA) compared to 22 percent of the same age cohort in the United States (OECD, 2015, p. 39). In fact, the OECD average for 25- to 64-year-olds holding BA degrees in the 30 member nations, representing some of the most industrialized nations around the globe, is only 16 percent, and the G20 average is 18 percent (OECD, 2015, p. 39).

The United States ranks 5th in the OECD with the percentage of students in the United States that finish some level of Tertiary education, whether it be two- or four-year degrees, when excluding international students. The United States ranks 7th when international students are included in the samples of all countries because the rankings of countries like Australia and New Zealand increase substantially due to the large amount of international students who earn degrees in those countries (OECD, 2015, p. 60). The United States ranks at the top of the world in terms of people aged 25 to 64 with doctorates (OECD, 2015, p. 39) and in the top 10 for people aged 22 to 34 with BA degrees.

The data on postsecondary degrees and other data presented earlier suggest that the overall education output as measured by multiple indicators increases when curriculum at the local level is less standardized. Education output also increases when a public school system is less standardized in its curriculum expectations and organized in a socio-civic manner that is open to all students in a democratic manner. Determining a child's academic and socio-civic future at age 13 only limits future possibilities for the child and depresses the overall education attainment and socio-civic and economic output of a nation.

For those who value a participative democracy in which people from all races, ethnicities, and social classes critique ideas, think creatively, and are able to lead, the historic purposes of public education are not to be dismissed as old-fashioned or rejected as no longer relevant. Dewey (1916) wrote that all citizens should participate actively in the democratic governing of the nation and the public school is the place where diverse peoples can become introduced to the American democratic traditions.

The public school is in essence the only social institution in the United States through which the vast majority of youth pass for an extended number of years. Thus, it is the only social institution in which the future generation of citizens can learn how to actively participate in the governing of their democratic country. The curriculum is the mechanism for socializing diverse groups of students into the American democratic experiment and for preparing them to address the problems that arise in a democracy and in the global community.

A problem of mass standardization is that it does not recognize the democratic traditions or functions of the public school because the programs and policies of standardization are authoritarian in nature, based on a top-down and singular vision of what it means to be globally competitive or academically prepared. Dewey (1938/1997) reminded readers that standardized authoritarian education has no place in a democratic society:

> The traditional scheme, is in essence, one of imposition from above and from outside. It imposes adult standards, subject-matter and methods upon those who are only moving slowly toward maturity. The gap is so great that the required subject-matter, the methods of learning and of behaving are foreign to the existing capacities of the young. . . . Consequently they must be imposed. (pp. 18–19)

The imposition of the standardized policies and practices is necessary because those policies and their outcomes are so far removed from democracy and so far removed from the evidence of how students learn best and how students learn to participate democratically in a global society that the policies and practices are not accepted by the general public. They must be forced upon the public.

The standardized policies and practices are generally developed by a small group of elites, distally from students and parents, and they are generally enacted through mandates or statutes. Standardized education then becomes based on the rule of ideology enforced via authoritarian regulations instead of democratic education focused on lifelong learning, discovery, and personal, cultural, and national growth. Dewey (1897) warned that authoritarian education reforms are doomed to failure:

> I believe that all reforms that rest simply on the enactment of a law or threatening of certain penalties or upon changes in the mechanical or outward arrangements are transitory and futile. (p. 80)

The more a reform violates the tenets of democratic participation and the ways that students learn best, the less effective and more detrimental to learning and democracy it becomes (Tanner and Tanner, 2007).

Avocational Function

A third historical purpose of public education has been the idea that public education has an avocational responsibility; it should help a person develop himself to a well-rounded human being so that he can improve his community, his culture, his country, and the larger global community (Commission on the Reorganization of Secondary Education, 1918). The pursuit of hobbies, passions, and interests that lie outside the economic realm help a person to become well rounded and diversified. Of course there are indirect benefits to the economic function of education when people are exposed to other pursuits. They generally become more cognitively nimble, culturally literate, personally satisfied, and socially conscious when exposed to diverse ideas and experiences (e.g., Aikin, 1942).

The development and specialization of the individual is not to be confused with individualism. One cannot lose sight of the big picture of democracy in terms of individuals contributing to the greater good of their local communities, larger American society, and the global community. Giles, McCutchen, and Zechiel (1942) warned of confusing individual development with individualism:

> In a democracy, however, the assumption is made that significant personalities can be developed only through the mutual sharing of interests and purposes.

> The development of the individual as a goal is not to be confused with individualistic action as a method for its achievement. Unrestrained individualism is inconsistent with democratic values since it will not guarantee others the realization of their potentialities . . . a sharing of responsibilities are essential for the development of personalities to their maximum. (p. 10)

The focus of the individual's development then is learning that there are responsibilities that individuals must assume in a democracy to ensure that the rights and liberties of all people are respected and protected. The development of one individual cannot impinge upon or retard the growth of another. "Individuals must learn that there are responsibilities, as well as advantages, in the sharing of concerns involved in group living" (Giles, McCutchen, and Zechiel, 1942, p. 10).

A person is not an island onto himself in a democracy. He has responsibilities to society to live respectfully and democratically.

Diversified Options

Regardless if one views the historic purposes of public education through two, three, or more functions, the fact remains that the purposes require a curriculum that provides opportunities for divergent thinking, divergent passions, and divergent interests based on the "needs of adolescents and seek to preserve and extend democracy as a way of life" (Giles, McCutchen, and Zechiel, 1942, p. 5). A comprehensive curriculum for a democratic public school system does not have the luxury of focusing only on a narrow band of routine academic skills and knowledge aimed at developing low-level workers and maintaining the social status quo. It must focus on cognitive, social, and emotional progress.

The curriculum should be unstandardized to create a diversity of expectations, ideas, and skills and not subjected to a recipe approach. The curricular program should recognize that "fundamental to individual development and to the refinement of democracy itself, is reliance upon the free play of intelligence in solving the problems of human concern" (Giles, McCutchen, and Zechiel, 1942, p. 10). The curriculum must attend to the multiple functions of public school in a democracy in a twenty-first-century innovation economy.

As Kerr (1999) noted, a comprehensive public school program should "try to identify essential human concerns. . . . In this kind of educational system, the primary focus of schools would be on human values, not economic utility" (p. 7). Preparing students to be economically sufficient is but one function among several for public schools. A guiding paradigm is necessary to help educators focus on the complementary functions of public school while simultaneously unstandardizing the curricular expectations to better meet the needs of students, their communities, the United States, and the global community.

THE CURRICULUM PARADIGM

Curriculum design, development, and implementation should be guided by a paradigm based on (a) evidence and experience for how students learn best and (b) the complementary functions of public school. Luckily, an evidence-informed paradigm for curriculum design, development, and implementation already exists. A paradigm is important for a professional field because it helps guide the evolution and growth of a profession and makes the profession less open to policies based on political expediency. Tanner and Tanner (2007) compared a paradigm to a compass in that the paradigm does not dictate the exact path, yet it provides a direction. A paradigm is not an endpoint, but a waypoint from which to navigate ideas and practices in the ongoing development of a profession.

An experimentalist-progressivist paradigm for curriculum was articulated and explained in detail by Tanner and Tanner (2007) and therefore not much space is taken here other than to provide a practical interpretation for those who have not read the original explanation. The presentation of a practical interpretation should not be taken to mean that the reader should not investigate and read the full details provided by Tanner and Tanner (2007).

The paradigm relates to (a) how students learn best, (b) theories of human development, (c) the most effective way to organize curriculum, and (d) general democratic and societal issues (Dewey, 1897). The Curriculum Paradigm is founded upon an experimentalist-progressivist philosophy of education, a philosophy of egalitarian and democratic progress through "reorganization of experiences which adds to the meaning of experience and which increases ability to direct the course of subsequent experiences" (Dewey, 1916/2009, p. 57).

The reorganization of experiences occurs through the use of methods for thinking. Specifically, the scientific method and related thinking processes are the basis for problem solving and critical and complex thinking. Critical and complex thinking should be embedded in a curriculum aligned to the paradigm and aimed at preparing students to be participative members of a democratic society in an uncertain future.

Experimental-progressivism is a purely American philosophy, made in the United States. It does not have its roots in the elitist European aristocracy and does not espouse or support cultural meritocracy. The philosophy does not view children as mini-adults nor as empty vessels into which knowledge is deposited from an adult who is in control of the education to a child in the role of passive receptacle. Progressive-experimentalism is a philosophy that supports active learning on the part of the child through democratic and reciprocal relationships between children, adults, content, experiences, skills, and dispositions. The child influences the curriculum as much as the curriculum influences the child.

Finding Direction

Returning to the idea of a paradigm as a compass, the progressive-experimentalist Curriculum Paradigm is a guide for educators and policy makers, not a recipe. The paradigm does not provide ready-made solutions because the challenges faced by public educators are not standardized, neatly packaged, or easy to address. The challenges faced by public educators are multifaceted, constantly evolving, and ill-structured. They are not standardized and cannot be solved by neatly packaged responses. As Tramaglini explained, "This isn't paint-by-numbers" referring to entrepreneurial and innovative leadership strategies and policy making required to address the diverse issues public educators are mandated to solve (personal communication, September 1, 2012).

There are no recipes to follow in order to create a comprehensive democratic education program. One cannot simply go through the motions to deal with the myriad issues thrust upon public schools. The power of the Curriculum Paradigm is that it provides direction so when educators do not know what to do exactly, they at least will have a direction to move toward, to align their policies and practices better with the paradigm. The paradigm provides a thinking guide, a way for educators to reflect upon their ideas to ensure the resulting policies and practices are more child-centered and evidence-informed.

This chapter interprets the paradigm as various parts, not in a linear manner, but interdependent like an ecosystem. Each part of the paradigm is presented one at a time only as a way to aid understanding and as a tool to organize ideas to guide curriculum development, design, and implementation. Readers should consider each facet as one part of a whole, supported by the progressivist-experimentalist philosophy, with all parts holding equal importance (see figure 5.1).

Parts of the Paradigm

Students learn best when provided with opportunities and experiences that recognize the nature of the learner (student) as an active constructor of meaning who brings life and academic experiences, interests, passions, emotions, and prior collateral knowledge to the classroom. The experiences and knowledge might be traditional or nontraditional, but no student is a passive blank

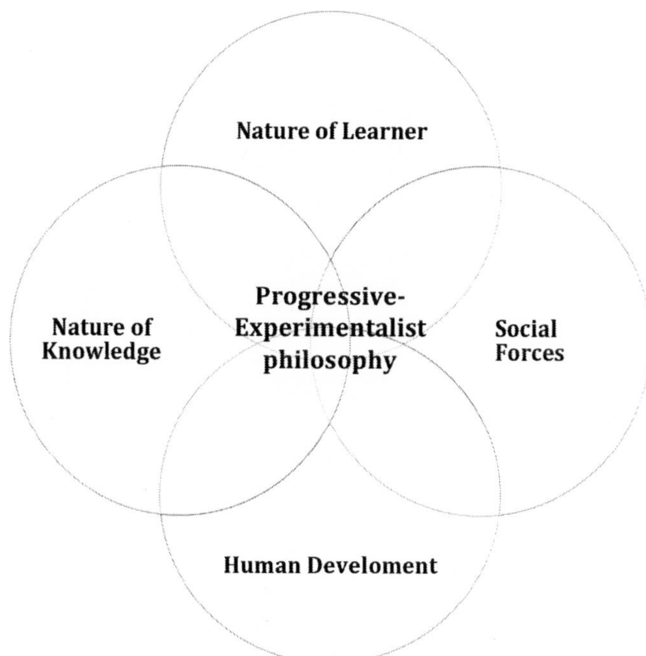

Figure 5.1 The Curriculum Paradigm. Adapted from Tanner, D. & Tanner, L. (2007). *Curriculum development: Theory into practice*. Upper Saddle River, NJ: Pearson.

slate or sponge (e.g., Dewey, 1902; 1938/1997; Thorndike, 1924; Tyler, 1949). School policies and practices should capitalize on opportunities to connect content to students through developmentally appropriate common experiences, interests, passions, and emotions to inform the content and organization of the curriculum.

Second, human development is not standardized. Student social, moral, and cognitive development is ongoing, fluid, and occurs in stages. It is not fixed (Dewey, 1902; Erikson, 1968; Havighurst, 1972; Kohlberg, 1970; Piaget, 1970; Woolfolk and Perry, 2011). Although there are general parameters for students to experience various stages of cognitive, moral, and social development, there are not finite cut-points in time, like the end of Grade 3 for instance, that all students can be expected to be at the same developmental stage. Also, not all students will attain mastery or advance through and up to the ultimate stages of development. For example, only approximately 40 percent of high school students can demonstrate mastery of abstract thinking (Tienken and Orlich, 2013).

The fact that not all students, or adults for that matter, master abstract thinking does not mean that high school students, or any other grade levels of students, should not have consistent opportunities to work in abstract situations, or that high school students or other grade levels cannot think abstractly. It simply means that a standardized expectation or requirement that all high school students will demonstrate mastery of abstract thinking would be inappropriate. Curriculum design, development, and implementation should account for diversity of human development and ultimate output.

Curriculum design, development, and implementation should be flexible by providing multiple pathways for students connect with content and demonstrate their level of readiness for mastery and understanding in relevant situations. For example, it is akin to the difference between all students connecting with Algebra II content versus all students being required to demonstrate the same level of mastery with Algebra II content in the same format, with the same emphasis, and identical level of difficulty. There is evidence for the value of connecting Algebra II content to all students, but there is no evidence for standardizing the curriculum expectations, emphasis, or output requirements (Marder, 2016).

Third, the curriculum, also known as the nature of knowledge, should be organized as a fusion of discipline-centered subject matter and personal/societal experiences, as the means to connect the content to the student (Taba, 1962; Tanner and Tanner, 2007). Authentic, ill-structured, divergent, socially conscious problem-solving situations that examine issues facing students in a democracy as members of a global community provide a basis for curriculum development, design, and implementation. The power of such curriculum organization is well known and demonstrated (e.g., Aikin, 1942).

Historically, socially conscious problem-based and project-based curricula programs produced better academic results as measured by traditional instruments such as standardized tests but also produced more socio-civic and avocational benefits (e.g., Jersild, Thorndike, and Goldman, 1939; 1941; Thorndike, 1924; Wrightstone, 1935). In most cases, the less standardized a school's curricula was in terms of problem-based and project-based opportunities and multiple pathways for students to demonstrate understanding, the better the results on academic and affective measures (Aikin, 1942; Wrightstone, Rechetnick, McCall, and Loftus, 1939).

The results from unstandardizing curriculum continued to be positive in the standardized education reform environment beginning in the late 1980s and beyond (e.g., Gijbels, Dochy, Van den Bossche, and Segers, 2005; Tramaglini and Tienken, 2016; Wang, Haertel, and Walberg, 1993). In general, the less standardized and more diversified a school's curriculum is, the better students perform on academic and nonacademic measures. Curriculum diversification and autonomy at the local level result in better education for students.

Fourth, democracy and local control are overriding cultural and social forces of public school and as such, public school is the incubator of democracy. Educating students for active, responsible participation in a democracy requires a democratic system of education and local control is a component of that system. Curriculum development, design, and implementation should be guided by principles of participatory democracy and connected to social forces. Equity, or the idea that one gets what he needs through diversification of curriculum and learning pathways that make a liberal education open to all, is an overriding facet of democratic life and should play a role in the design, development, and implementation of curricula.

If one uses the progressive-experimentalist Curriculum Paradigm as a compass for action, curriculum development, design, and implementation become more like a fluid process focused on students and experiential education rather than a static product. Curriculum development becomes a process of ongoing evolution toward greater progress academically and socially when guided by the paradigm, and not simply an endpoint of unquestioned efficiency.

Thus, curricula design, development, and implementation, if guided by the evidence-informed paradigm, would not be standardized and static. Instead, curricula would be diverse and pliable and allow for multiple pathways for learning and demonstrating learning. The paradigm helps educators to focus on the maturation of the whole child, cognitive, social, and emotional, as encouraged by Civil War colonel and teacher, Francis W. Parker, whom Dewey called the father of progressive education.

Using the Paradigm

The practical utility of the paradigm is such that it can help educators and those concerned about attending to the complementary functions of a robust public school system to make better decisions about programs and policies and limit long-term harm to students. Educators and officials responsible for curriculum design, development, policy, and implementation need only filter their ideas through the various facets of the paradigm and look for areas that are less aligned with the four facets.

For instance, reforms, programs, or policies based on standardized ideology that treat curriculum as mere subject-matter information to be absorbed and regurgitated by the learner on a high-stakes state-mandated test put students in the mode of passive receptacle of information and certainly violate the nature of the learner and the nature of knowledge as a fusion of subject matter and personal connections. Policies and practices that have heavily departed from the Curriculum Paradigm have always failed to achieve their advertised results (Tanner and Tanner, 2007).

Policy makers can use the paradigm to guide their decision-making regarding mandates and solutions. They can conduct a potential problem analysis on their ideas for the short term and long term through the lenses of the Paradigm and ask four basic questions: (1) How does the policy facilitate education practices that empower students to be active constructors of meaning and respect their prior knowledge and experiences? (2) How does the policy facilitate the development of curriculum that represents a fusion of subject matter to student experiences, interests, and passions? (3) How does this policy facilitate practices that can respect the natural cognitive, social, and emotional differences that exist among students? (4) How does this policy allow for the democratic development and implementation of the practices related to it?

Educators can use the Paradigm to help evaluate existing school-level policies and practices. They can revise current policies and practices to align more with aspects of the paradigm. Because the Curriculum Paradigm is an evidence-informed and practice-proven tool, educators can use it as a holistic rubric to reflect upon their policies and practices. For example, educators that mandate all students take "drill and skill" test preparation courses might notice that type of course and policy violates the way students learn best and the best ways to organize curriculum. Such a mandate is also not a democratic way to run a school.

Similarly, educators can use the Paradigm as a guide when they develop new school-level policies and practices or customize existing policies that violate it. Educators can become policy and practice designers and innovators by using the underlying ideas of the Paradigm to help design or revise, as best they can given their current contexts, policies and practices that align to the facets of the paradigm. The paradigm can provide educators with ideas or the educational compass they need to make small tweaks or changes that can help them creatively reduce the harm of existing bad policies and practices.

The current fetish with mandated statewide standardize testing is an example of a policy and a practice that educators at the local level do not control, but they can use the Paradigm to reduce some of the negative effects to students.Simple actions such as (a) do not mandate static, isolated test preparation activities for children; (b) embed important skills and concepts into the curriculum through integrated problem-based activities that connect student interests and prior knowledge to content, instead of isolated curriculum related to the test; (c) provide accurate information about the strengths and weaknesses of the testing as opposed to parroting the state-developed sound bites that often include misinformation; (d) deal democratically and humanely with students and parents who choose to not have their children take such assessments; and (e) do not voluntarily use the results from one standardized test to make important decisions about students.

Parents, guardians, and community members can use the Paradigm as a structure and tool when evaluating sometimes-amorphous federal, state, and local policies and practices. It provides non-educators with a way to make sense of seemingly disconnected policies and it also provides them with some research-based tools and language to use when asking questions or making suggestions. The world of education policy and advocating for appropriate policies can seem overwhelming without some type of tool to help clarify the landscape. The Curriculum Paradigm is one tool.

Which Knowledge?

Inevitably the argument about curriculum standards and standardization always returns to Spencer's (1883) basic question about what knowledge is of most worth. Not only have policy makers and educators struggled to provide a unified answer to Spencer's question, they have also struggled to find the right mix between which knowledge, how much emphasis should be placed on specific types and forms of knowledge, and what is considered "common" knowledge among an educated citizenry.

Goodlad (1983) described the tension around Spencer's questions and gave a clue to a possible solution:

> But this still leaves us with the issues of what and how much is to be encountered commonly and of how much of what is to be generally common is to be specifically common. One can argue persuasively that all citizens should understand something about the history of their country, but what is this "something" and must everyone encounter all of it? If "some" is enough, when does just some become not enough? It begins to become obvious that the answers to these and related questions are relative; they never will be answered absolutely or finally. (p. 303)

Although proponents of standardization might believe they can accurately decide what knowledge should be commonly known now and what will be worth most in the future, as well as determine the amount of specificity, emphasis, and the format for that knowledge, Goodlad (1983) reminded educators that it is not possible to do so. The United States and the larger global community are diverse demographically, culturally, and economically. The passions, interests, skills, and knowledge valued and useful in one region or one economic sector might be less so in another. Yet it is those same diverse interests, passions, cultures, knowledge, and skills of the approximately 320 million people that live in the United States that make it one of the most cognitively and economically nimble countries in the world.

It is not possible or warranted to provide just one answer to Spencer's question for a public school system that serves approximately 56 million children with a global community of over 7 billion people. The answer depends on context. Thus, a less standardized system of locally controlled public schools, with a majority of the curriculum locally developed and customized, yet globally informed, is the answer.

UNSTANDARDIZED ATTRIBUTES FOR THE FUTURE

Standardization feels safe. It is a straightforward, linear concept and makes complex issues seem alluringly simple. It is a tempting solution to an ill-structured problem. It is easier to allow a national commission or presidentially appointed committee decide which knowledge is of most worth than to engage in the ongoing, messy, inefficient processes of deciding those things locally and democratically.

But policies and practices that seek to standardize curricular expectations and outputs fail to recognize the specific complementary functions of public school, nor do they recognize the fundamental purpose of education in general: changing the ways human beings behave, think, and feel about themselves and others, as members of a global community. Smith and Tyler (1942) explained that the general purpose of education must be broad in scope, and unstandardized in methods and outputs:

> The fundamental purpose of an education is to effect changes in the behavior of the student, that is, in the way he thinks, and feels, and acts. . . . Basically, the goals of education represent these changes in human beings which we hope to bring about through education. The kinds of ideas which we expect students to get and to use, the kinds of skills which we hope they will develop, the techniques of thinking which we hope they will acquire, the ways in which we hope they will learn to react to esthetic experiences; these are illustrations of educational objectives. (pp. 11–12)

The simplistic notions embedded in standardization and the corresponding theory of performativity focus solely on methods and procedures and the degree of sameness in the outputs. Those notions are not appropriate for educating students as members of a global society in an uncertain future. The words of Smith and Tyler serve as a reminder that quality education is unstandardized. It is about big ideas, lifelong changes, and skills and dispositions that transcend time and place.

The primitive ideas and ideologies of standardization must be jettisoned in order to prepare students to be participative, economically stable, and contributing stewards of a democracy and responsible members of a global society. After one mentally moves past the seeming security and alluring simplicity of standardization and performativity, many creative and innovative ideas become visible. Curriculum can be organized around skills and dispositions that transcend subject matter, time, and international boundaries and attend to the complementary functions of public school.

There is a need for unstandardized skills and dispositions such as active listening, big-picture thinking, cognitive nimbleness, collaboration, communicating, compassion, compromise, confidence, conscientiousness, consensus building, courage, creativity, critique, critical consideration of information, cultural literacy, curiousness, dignity, divergent thinking, empathy, entrepreneurial thinking, environmental stewardship, ethics, fairness, friendship, goal setting, happiness, humility, imagination, innovation, integrity, kindness, leadership, love, motivation, networking building, openness, persistence, potential problem analysis, pride, problem finding, problem solving, reflection, resilience, self-control, self-efficacy, sharing, social consciousness, strategizing, taking action, timeliness, worldliness, and visioning (see table 5.1).

Those are skills and dispositions worth developing in students. Those are the skills and dispositions that will serve students for the rest of their lives. There are certainly more skills and dispositions that could be added, and their meanings can be better defined by simply reading up on the literature of each, but the preceding list provides examples of unstandardized dispositions and skills that draw upon the past, inform the present, and prepare for the future.

Table 5.1 Unstandardized Skills and Dispositions for an Uncertain Future

Active listening	Divergent thinking	Openness
Big-picture thinking	Empathy	Persistence
Cognitive nimbleness	Entrepreneurial thinking	Potential problem analysis
Collaboration	Environmental stewardship	Pride
Communicating	Ethics	Problem finding
Compassion	Fairness	Problem solving
Compromise	Friendship	Reflection
Confidence	Goal setting	Resilience
Conscientiousness	Happiness	Self-control
Consensus building	Humility	Self-efficacy
Courage	Imagination	Sharing
Creativity	Innovation	Social consciousness
Critical consideration of information	Integrity	Strategizing
	Kindness	Taking action
Critique	Leadership	Timeliness
Cultural literacy	Love	Visioning
Curiousness	Motivation	Worldliness
Dignity	Network building	

The skills and dispositions in table 5.1 can form the basis for unstandardized curriculum design, development, and implementation to defy standardization. Students can experience curriculum developed, designed, and implemented from an evidence-informed position that fosters the development of *future-necessary* skills and dispositions via policies, programs, and practices aligned to the Curriculum Paradigm. The future-necessary skills and dispositions can be developed through democratic means and decided upon locally.

The skills and dispositions listed in table 5.1 are considered unstandardized because their products and outputs can take many forms, as can the assessments used to gage student demonstration. The skills and dispositions are hard to quantify and some are hard to define in precise terms. Yet, they are all important for thriving in an uncertain future. They represent what some call the intangible skills or the soft skills, although there is nothing soft about them.

They are the skills and dispositions that set the creative apart from the common, the innovative from imitative, and leaders from followers. Standardized academic automatons are like one trick ponies if they do not possess unstandardized skills and dispositions. They have knowledge but no way of using it or communicating it in ways that result in positive and useful actions or outcomes for themselves or others. Academic automatons are imitators, not creators.

Of course there is traditional academic content that needs to be integrated with the unstandardized dispositions and skills. There is no shortage of ideas for what that traditional content might consist of with a comprehensive curricular program. For example, the subject domain of mathematics has existed for a very long time. The idea presented here is that based on the Curriculum Paradigm, the content common to each grade level would be developed locally, informed from local, regional, state, national, and global sources, and evolved from local priorities, interests, passions, wants, needs, assessments of the future, dreams, and multiple sources of evidence. The time devoted to and emphasis on the various dispositions, content, and skills would be determined locally.

Difficulty Versus Complexity

There seems to be some confusion on the part of proponents of standardization about the differences between difficulty and complexity as related to high-level thinking. The higher-level skills and dispositions necessary for the future are developed via experiences that provide students opportunities to engage with complex learning objectives and to use complex thinking. Unstandardized curriculum designed, developed, and implemented aligned with the Curriculum Paradigm, and based on an experimentalist-progressivist philosophy, uses problem-solving and critical thinking frameworks to connect complex content to students.

But that is not the case with past and current standardized curricular programs and reforms. Those programs and reforms use contrived difficulty to masquerade as higher-level and complex thinking. Given the theoretical and philosophical foundations of standardization, the use of difficulty instead of complexity makes sense. Difficult content is not necessarily complex.

The reader might recall from the previous chapter that the theory of performativity and the curricular philosophy of Essentialism dominate standardized thinking. Both value effort over interest. As stated, the mindset used in standardized curricular programs is "no pain, no gain" and as such curricula objectives need to be considered difficult to be in the words of Spencer (1883) "of most worth."

As explained in a study that compared the complexity of the high school CCSS to the former New Jersey high school standards, complexity and difficulty are necessary components of a comprehensive curriculum, but the complexity of a learning objective is something that is dynamic and multidimensional in nature (Sforza, Tienken, and Kim, 2016). Sousa (2011) explained complexity as the thought processes required to address a given task, a set of tasks, or a problem.

One can think of complexity as the difference between remembering a fact or imitating a procedure and developing an original product, process, or solution. Regurgitating facts and imitating procedures are less cognitively complex than developing an original product or process, yet both are necessary components of a curriculum.

"Difficulty is a more static component of a learning objective that simply refers to the amount of work or effort a student must use to complete a task, regardless of complexity" (Sforza, Tienken, and Kim, p. 9). For example, the following two learning objectives illustrate differences in difficulty while providing relatively similar levels of complexity: (1) Students will be able to apply the standard algorithm to solve problems involving three-digit numbers multiplied by two-digit numbers; and (2) students will be able to apply the standard algorithm to solve problems involving three-digit numbers multiplied by three-digit numbers.

Requiring students to solve a multiplication problem in which a three-digit number is multiplied by a two-digit number is less difficult than solving a problem in which a three-digit number is multiplied by another three-digit number. The complexity remains at the recall and procedural levels, but the second objective is theoretically more difficult because it requires more effort, more work, to multiply more numbers. The processes to arrive at the predetermined, convergent solutions are already known or specified for both objectives. One objective simply requires more steps, and thus more effort.

The students are required to more or less apply the same type of thinking to arrive at the solution.

Conversely, the following objective, adapted from the Graduation Performance System (GPS) developed by the Asia Society (2015), represents complex thinking: *Students will take a position based on evidence from sources that considers multiple cultural perspectives and draw actionable conclusions on a globally significant issue/topic*. The objective is complex in nature and requires divergent thinking. There are not predetermined solutions at which students must arrive or a narrow set of processes they must use to arrive at a solution. There is not a recipe to follow.

The complex and divergent nature of the objective provides for more opportunities for students to engage in the development and use of the future-necessary skills and dispositions noted earlier. Students must integrate knowledge and skills, and in some cases even create or synthesize new knowledge and ideas to address the complex objective. Making students perform mental acrobatics is not complex or unstandardized thinking. That is wasting time and money on contrived difficulty.

Next Steps

Although some might not be able to make sense of the diverse nature of American public education, locally controlled, nonstandardized education is one hallmark of our democracy. Conant (1958) described it in the following terms:

> The doctrine of local responsibility and community independence can be related to our pioneer history without difficulty. Parish and county autonomy in the South, the seventeenth-century independence of New England church congregations, and the suspicion of centralized government are among the factors that shaped the present political structure of our school system in many states. Yet there is no uniform structure. (p. 9)

Likewise, locally controlled, nonstandardized curriculum development is not expedient because democracy and the processes used to develop unstandardized curricula that address social issues are not expedient. Educators should not be made to sacrifice effectiveness for expediency, because what is expedient is not always effective. The message here is not that curriculum should not extend, challenge, and enrich students. On the contrary, it should. And it should engage students in complex thinking and span multiple cognitive developmental stages at each grade level to ensure equity: all children getting what they need, not all getting the same. Complexity and unstandardized skills and dispositions, not contrived difficulty and static knowledge accumulation, are necessary components to design curricula for an uncertain future in a democratic country and global community.

The early twentieth-century Italian pedagogist Guissipina Pizzigoni (1914) echoed Parker's (1894) and Dewey's (1899) calls for a guiding vision of curriculum and pedagogy that provides students diverse experiences to evolve as individuals as part of a larger democratic society. Pizzigoni stated that the school must teach us to live together and among the many challenges that life presents: that is why school has to look like a small society, where individuals are free to fulfill their duty. So although progressive-experimentalism is an American invention, the essence of the philosophy has come to germinate seeds of democratic and unstandardized education in other cultures.

The next two chapters present ideas and specific example on how to begin to defy standardization in the current standardized environment. The reader should interpret the ideas presented as food for thought, not the recipe. Concrete examples are provided for readers to consider and use to conceptualize strategies to begin unstandardizing their current education context for students.

REFERENCES

Aikin, W.M. (1942). *The story of the eight-year study*. New York: Harper.

Asia Society. (2015). *Graduation performance system*. Author. Retrieved from http://asiasociety.org/competence/leadership-global-competence.

Commission on the Reorganization of Secondary Education. (1918). *Cardinal principles of secondary education*. Washington, DC: U.S. Bureau of Education, Bulletin No. 35.

Conant, J.B. (1958). *The American high school today*. New York: McGraw-Hill Book Company.

Dewey, J. (1897). My pedagogic creed. *School Journal, 54*, 77–80.

Dewey, J. (1899). *School and society*. Chicago: University of Chicago. Original publication date.

Dewey, J. (1902). *The child and the curriculum*. Chicago: University of Chicago Press.

Dewey, J. (1916). *Democracy and education*. New York: McMillan.

Dewey, J. (1916/2009). *Democracy and education: An introduction to the philosophy of education*. Cedar Lake, MI: Readaclassic.

Dewey, J. (1929) Sources of science in education. New York: Liveright, p. 84. (From the forward to *The Use of Resources in Education* by Elise Ripley Clapp, 1952, Harper.)

Dewey, J. (1938/1997). *Experience and education*. New York: Touchstone.

Erikson, E.H. (1968). *Identity: Youth in crisis*. New York: Norton.

Gijbels, D., Dochy, F., Van den Bossche, P., & Segers, M. (2005). Effects of problem-based learning: A meta-analysis from the angle of assessment. *Review of Educational Research, 75*(1), 27–61.

Giles, H.H., McCutchen, S.P., & Zechiel, A.N. (1942). *Adventures in American education volume II: Exploring the curriculum.* New York: Harper and Brothers.

Goodlad, J. (1983). Diversity, commonality, and practice. In K.J. Rehage, G.D. Fenstermacher, & J. Goodlad, (Eds.), *Individual differences and the common curriculum.* National Society of Education (NSSE), 82nd Annual Yearbook, Part I. Chicago: University of Chicago.

Havighurst, R.J. (1972) *Developmental tasks and education.* Philadelphia, PA: McKay.

Jersild, A.T., Thorndike, R.L., & Goldman, B. (1939). An evaluation of aspects of the activity program in New York City elementary schools. *Journal of Experimental Education, 8*, 166–207.

Jersild, A.T., Thorndike, R.L., & Goldman, B. (1941). A further comparison of pupils in "activity" and "non-activity" schools. *Journal of Experimental Education, 9*, 307–309.

Kerr, S.T. (Ed.). (1999). Visions of sugarplums: The future of technology, education, and the schools. In *Technology and the future of schooling. 95th yearbook of the National Society for the study of education, Part II.* Chicago: University of Chicago Press.

Kohlberg, L. (1970). Education for justice. In J.M. Gustafson (Ed.), *Moral education* (pp. 57–65). Cambridge, MA: Harvard University Press.

Marder, M. (2016). High school mathematics in Texas: Freedom and shackles. In C. Tienken & C. Mullen (Eds.), *Education policy perils: Tackling the tough issues* (pp. 134–156). Philadelphia, PA: Taylor Francis Routledge.

OECD. (2015). Education at a glance. OECD indicators. OECD Publishing. Retrieved from http://www.keepeek.com/Digital-Asset-Management/oecd/education/education-at-a-glance-2015_eag-2015-en#page1.

Parker, F.W. (1894). *Talks on pedagogics.* New York: E.L. Kellog.

Piaget, J. (1970). *Science of education and the psychology of the child* (D. Coltman, Trans.). New York: Orion.

Pizzigoni, G. (1914). *La Scuola Elementare Rinnovata secondo il Metodo Sperimentale* [The elementary school reimagined according to the experimental method]. Milano, IT: G.B. Paravia & Co.

Sforza, D., Tienken, C.H., & Kim, E. (2016). A comparison of higher-order thinking in the grades 9–12 Common Core State Standards and the 2009 New Jersey content standards for English language arts and mathematics. *AASA Journal of Scholarship and Practice, 12*(4), 4–32.

Smith & Tyler, R. (1942). *Adventures in American education volume III: Appraising and recording student progress.* New York: Harper and Brothers.

Sousa, D. (2011). *How the brain learns* (4th Ed.). Thousand Oaks, CA: Corwin.

Spencer, H. (1883). What knowledge is of most worth? (Originally published in 1859). In *Education: Intellectual moral, and physical, Chapter 1,* pp. 1–96. New York: Appleton.

Taba, H. (1962). *Curriculum development: Theory into practice.* New York: Harcourt, Brace, & World, Inc.

Tanner, D. & Tanner, L. (2007). *Curriculum development: Theory into practice.* Upper Saddle River, NJ: Pearson.

Thorndike, E.L. (1924). Mental discipline in high school studies. *Journal of Educational Psychology, 15*, 1–22, 98.

Tienken, C.H. & Orlich, D.C. (2013). *The school reform landscape: Fraud, myth, and lies*. New York: Rowman and Littlefield.

Tramaglini, T.W. & Tienken, C.H. (2016). Customized curriculum and high achievement in high poverty schools. In C. Tienken & C. Mullen (Eds.), *Education policy perils: Tackling the tough issues* (pp. 75–101). Philadelphia, PA: Taylor Francis Routledge.

Tyler, R. W. (1949). *Basic principles of curriculum and instruction*. Chicago: University of Chicago Press.

Woolfolk, A. & Perry, N.E. (2011). *Child and adolescent development*. Upper Saddle River, NJ: Pearson.

Wang, M.C., Haertel, G.D., & Walberg, H.J. (1993). Toward a knowledge base for school learning. *Review of Educational Research, 63*(3), 249–294.

Wrightstone, J.W. (1935). *Appraisal of newer practices in selected public schools*. New York: Teachers College Press.

Wrightstone, J.W., Rechetnick, J., McCall, W.A., & Loftus, J.J. (1939). Measuring social performance factors in activity control schools of New York City. *Teachers College Record, 40*(5), 423–432.

Chapter 6

Unstandardized Beginnings

Theory into Action

The processes, methods, and pathways for the development of curricula that includes the knowledge, complexity, skills, and dispositions necessary for an uncertain future in a global community are by nature unstandardized. There are many pathways educators, parents, and students can use to create engaging curricula that align to the Curriculum Paradigm, address the complementary functions of public school, and defy standardization.

This chapter provides evidence-informed ideas derived from some of public education's landmark studies and iconic thinkers on ways to structure and enhance less standardized curriculum for all students, regardless of the bureaucratically mandated standards that are in place. The chapter includes the decided use of direct quotations from some the progressive-experimentalist giants in the curriculum field to add historical support and authentic voice to the ideas presented herein.

The use of the classical literature and direct quotations is purposeful to (a) provide readers with evidence-informed suggestions to dismantle standardized curriculum expectations faced by public educators, parents, and students; (b) illustrate that many of the challenges posed by standardization are not new and they occurred before; (c) explain how unstandardized, evidenced-informed solutions were developed and implemented by progressive-experimentalist educators with great success; and (d) provide current educators with concrete suggestions, based on demonstrated track-records of success, to defy standardization.

Practice without knowledge of what one is practicing begets imitation, not creation and innovation. When the only tool one has is a hammer, everything looks like a nail. The suggestions in this chapter provide educators with more tools so that they use the hammer of standardization less often on students.

INFORMED CURRICULUM DEVELOPMENT

The ideas and examples presented in this chapter comport with Dewey's (1916/2009, pp. 88–91) proposal that curriculum is something that needs to be transformed into usable, transferable knowledge by the educator and students through a process of reorganization, reconstruction, and reflection. The ideas and examples also align with the definition of curriculum used earlier in this book as the "reconstruction of knowledge and experience that enables the learner to grow in exercising intelligent control of subsequent knowledge and experience" (Tanner and Tanner, 2007, p. 99).

Recipes, quick-fix promises and proclamations, junk science, or over-the-top claims of miracle cure-alls for whatever problems seem to be ailing a local education agency and public education in general are noticeably absent in the chapter. It is the professional responsibility of the reader to artfully, creatively, and innovatively apply the ideas and the research presented. There are no standardized solutions being vended here. Innovative, socially conscious, and entrepreneurial leadership are necessary to defy standardization and create curricula all children deserve. Unquestionably following the standardized pack will not get the job done.

There is no such thing as "Educator Proof" curriculum, nor should there be. Organizing and implementing curriculum for development of the unstandardized skills and dispositions presented in chapter 5 is an organic process that cannot be micromanaged or distally programmed in ways that limit teacher, parent, and student input. Education automatons cannot unstandardize education. The focus of curriculum policy and leadership should be to facilitate the democratic curricula processes that relate to the Curriculum Paradigm and that address the complementary functions of public school. Educators, parents, and students should not be separated from the processes of design, development, and implementation of curricula.

Curriculum design, development, and implementation are iterative processes. There should be constant evolution based on reflection akin to the definition of curriculum presented in the beginning of this book and Dewey's conception of curriculum as "reorganization of experiences which adds to the meaning of experience and which increases ability to direct the course of subsequent experiences" (Dewey, 1916/2009, p. 57). Unquestionably following a standardized pathway is not an acceptable option. Leadership is required.

NATURE OF KNOWLEDGE: ORGANIZE TO UNSTANDARDIZE

Function follows form in many cases in education. Curriculum must be created and organized in ways that lead to the development of unstandardized skills and dispositions needed for an uncertain future. For example, if greater facilitation of creative, innovative, and socially conscious thinking are desired goals, then the local curriculum should include purposeful activities and integrated problem-based units designed by educators and students to achieve those goals. Lip service, rhetoric, one-size-fits-all programs, or false promises will not produce the desired outcomes.

The way knowledge is organized, via the locally designed, customized, and implemented written curricula influences the way educators plan classroom curricula and engage in teaching and assessment. The way the curricula is organized influences how students experience the curriculum in terms of how and what they learn. Different curricular structures yield different student experiences and ultimately influence their outcomes. Curriculum written in an isolated, subject-centered, or a disciplinary manner is less likely to lead to activities that foster creative, innovative, action-oriented, and big-picture thinking than curriculum that seeks to integrate knowledge, skills, and dispositions for the ultimate purpose of transferring them to real-world issues.

General, concrete principles for the development of unstandardized curriculum are borrowed from Volume II of the Eight-Year Study and other landmark works of curriculum development and evaluation (Giles, McCutchen, and Zechiel, 1942, p. 121). The authors of Volume II of the Eight-Year Study described four principles for consideration based on a key component of the Curriculum Paradigm that students must be active participants in learning:

> With the belief that we learn by doing and that growth, to be permanent, is best achieved through experience, the procedure of the educational process is as follows:
>
> 1. analysis by each individual, on his own maturation level, of his needs and his interests in accordance with the best obtainable standards of social relationships;
> 2. defining of possible goals on the basis of these needs and interests;
> 3. participation in experiences that offer opportunity for growth toward the desirable goals;
> 4. evaluation in terms of this growth on the part of students, parents and teachers.

The four principles acknowledge that students are active constructors of meaning influenced by the curriculum and who exert influence upon it. The curriculum should provide opportunities for students to act and reflect on their needs, interests, and social development through content and experiences related to them. The principles suggest that students and educators must have authentic choice and voice in the design, development, and implementation of the curriculum in ways that provide for developmentally appropriate goals and objectives. Students and educators learn from curricular experiences and the curriculum evolves and is customized based on student and educator experiences, passions, and interests. It is a living document that can be revised before, during, and after implementation.

The above principles provide a general road map toward a system for overcoming, subverting, and dismantling standardization through the development of unstandardized curriculum. The principles suggest that educators provide opportunities for student introspection of their current developmental needs and interests followed by the definition of cognitive and social-emotional learning aims based on that introspection (see figure 6.1). Planned learning experiences follow learning aims.

Students' results from the learning experience are subject to review, during and after the experiences, by multiple parties, including the students, to obtain a scrap-book approach, or multiple-methods approach to student and educator evaluation and feedback. The feedback obtained informs the ongoing experiences and the formative introspection that takes place on the part of students and educators, creating an ongoing feedback loop.

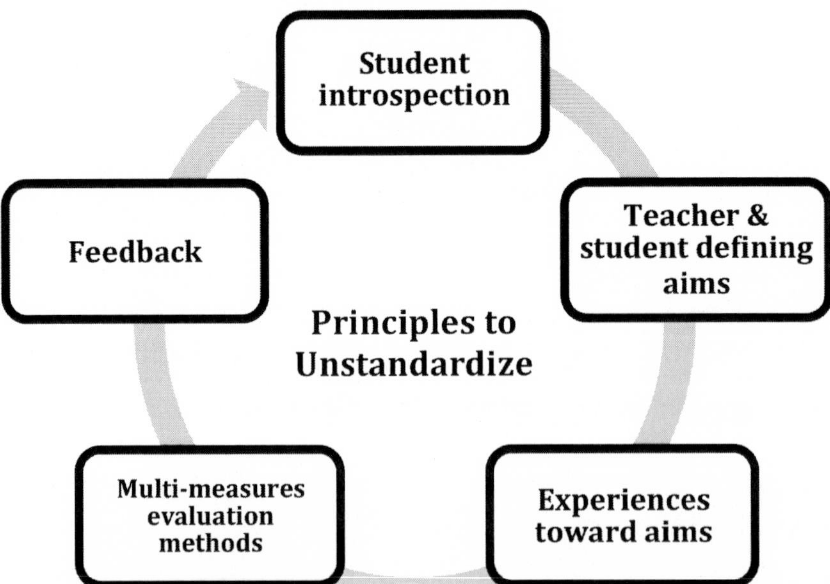

Figure 6.1 The Principles to Unstandardize. Adapted from Giles, H.H., McCutchen, S.P., & Zechiel, A.N. (1942). *Adventures in American education volume II: Exploring the curriculum.* New York: Harper and Brothers.

STRUCTURES FOR ORGANIZATION

One direction from which to begin evolving the general principles depicted in figure 6.1 into less standardized curricula that address the complementary functions of public school while simultaneously aligning to the Curriculum Paradigm is to use high-interest, realistic problems based on societal demands and personal needs of students as the basis for curricular units. Socially conscious problems are an effective vehicle to operationalize the unstandardizing process regardless of the curricula and programs currently in place in an education context. Irrespective of how one conceives of a unit of study, whether short term or long term, broad or specific, problem-based units are a superior structure from which to organize curricula.

The educational context itself is part of the consideration when designing, developing, and implementing curricula. Dewey (1916/2009) recommended that selection of a problem for study must be "an outgrowth of existing conditions. It must be based upon a consideration of what is already going on; upon the resources and difficulties of the situation" (p. 75). Dewey's advice helps educators to ensure that student interest and needs are incorporated into the socially conscious unit of study. The selection of a problem based on careful consideration of what is already occurring in society addresses a pressing social force, and aligns with another important aspect of the Curriculum Paradigm such as the nature of the learner as an active constructor of meaning.

In the final analysis, a curriculum is the vehicle to organize knowledge, skills, and dispositions for students to experience. The organization and implementation of the written curricula matter greatly in terms of how students learn and how they transfer the learning to meaningful actions. The standardized, discipline-centered, isolated subjects approach is less likely to develop the necessary unstandardized skills and dispositions in students who do not naturally possess them or children who have them hidden below the surface of their minds and outward personalities. Collecting facts and isolated skills for regurgitation on a standardized test does not satisfy students' natural curiosity and drive to experience life, learn, and to actively apply their learning to influence life situations.

The ways students come to experience and influence knowledge, skills, and dispositions and the choice and voice they have in the processes, influence the experienced curriculum in the classroom and beyond. As Caldwell (1927) stated when describing the Lincoln Experimental School, the organization of the curriculum around socially conscious problems is of interest to students and society because it, "arouses questions, stimulates thought, and calls for the development of more knowledge. Education is the great dissatisfier, the great arouser of ambitions and needs not previously known" (p. 273).

The use of socially conscious problems, of interest to students, to organize curricula has a demonstrated history of leading to deeper learning. Pursuing socially conscious problems provides more opportunities for students to transfer their knowledge to contribute to personal and community growth while learning skills, knowledge, and dispositions necessary for economic viability and life in a democratic society and global community. Learning is more active and less static when based on socially conscious problems.

Results from a series of landmark studies suggest that students involved in unstandardized, problem-focused, curricular programs outperform peers in traditional, standardized programs, academically, socially, and civically (e.g., Jersild, Thorndike, and Goldman, 1941; Thorndike, 1924; Wrightstone, Rechetnick, McCall, and Loftus, 1939; Wrightstone, 1935). More recent studies demonstrated that locally customized curricula based on problems and projects leads to higher academic achievement, even when mandated state curricula standards exist and achievement is measured via standardized tests (e.g., Wang, Haertel, and Walberg, 1993). More students learn more when curricula is unstandardized, especially students from poverty (e.g., Tramaglini and Tienken, 2016). The time to argue that standardizing is a superior solution to the problems that ail education is long past. It is time to defy standardization.

PROBLEM FINDING

Developmentally appropriate, socially conscious problems of high interest to students and educators have a greater potential of arousing student inquiry, tapping their ambitions to succeed, lead, and act for the greater good, and their drive to go beyond the written curriculum to discover new knowledge, critique existing ideas, and create knowledge. Giles, McCutchen, and Zechiel (1942) commented:

> The use of problems which are real and which are understood by the students engage their sympathy and enthusiasm from the beginning. This, furthermore, makes it possible for the students to see the value of what they are doing, and to learn how to evaluate their own work. Self-evaluation, in turn, leads to a desire to learn the things that are necessary for greater achievement. (p. 115)

The use of developmentally appropriate, socially conscious problems as a general curricular structure is an evidence-informed and concrete way for educators to begin to organize knowledge for study. Problems are also effective means for students to encounter unstandardized skills and dispositions and ultimately learn and transfer them for use in authentic contexts in intelligent and responsible ways in order to grow as individuals and contribute to the greater good. Caldwell (1927) cited general psychological principles when he stressed the need for developmentally appropriate problems, experiences, and expectations to support cognitive and emotional growth and transfer of learning when he wrote "Children develop fastest when engaged most of the time in doing things they can do—not constantly failing in things they cannot do" (p. 277).

Although not to be widely circulated for another fifty years, Caldwell may well have been channeling Vygotsky's (1978) concept of *Zone of Proximal Development*. Vygotsky (1978) suggested that students can access and work with challenging content, vis-à-vis socially conscious problems, with the guidance of an educator, through carefully planned and scaffolded guided practice and independent experiences. Success breeds success. Evidence-based problem-solving methods for the implementation of curricula can flow from the socially conscious problems, as can the reciprocal analyses of the problems associated with the student solutions to those problems (Achilles, Reynolds, and Achilles, 1997).

How can educators and students find socially conscious problems? In general, problem finding is concerned with helping people accurately identify and define problems instead of merely uncovering topics or facts, or identifying a problem so broadly as to inhibit deep study (Achilles, Reynolds, and Achilles, 1997). Problem finding is part of the overall process of problem analysis (Achilles, Reynolds, and Achilles, 1997). In the context of unstandardized curriculum design, development, and implementation educators can begin the problem finding process with students within developmentally appropriate, socially conscious topics suggested by students and educators.

The starter themes listed below, also known as general ideas, were generated by a group of elementary school students, aged eight to ten, during a five-minute brainstorming session, on things they were concerned with in the world, their country, and their community. The teacher facilitated the session with some basic parameters and an example of some socially conscious themes at each level of concern, and then asked the students to collaboratively think and make suggestions. The teacher prompted and refined student thinking with probing and clarifying questions to arrive at the following list of themes:

> Pollution, Climate Change, Economics and Earning a Living, Immigration, Poverty, Homelessness, Cost of Living, Bullying, Greed, Animal Rights, Global Citizenship, Endangered Wildlife, Population Growth, Personal Relationships, Personal Rights, Government and Peoples, Communities, Sanitation, Energy Supplies.

Funneling toward the Problem

Below is an example of a funnel approach to thinking that educators can use to facilitate and refine student thinking from general themes to more specific topics. The example presented herein was used with elementary school students to help them narrow broad ideas from a theme to a more specific topic on the way toward finding a socially conscious problem from which to organize curriculum activities (see figure 6.2). The approach is similar to one used with doctoral candidates to help them identify potential research topics.

The funnel illustrated in figure 6.2 began with students identifying the high-interest, broad theme of pollution. The process ended with students settling upon the Great Pacific Garbage Patch as their socially conscious topic for study. Students funneled from a broad theme to a specific topic embedded within their high-interest theme. But the topic is not the problem. It is a place to begin finding problems. For example, it is a fact that the Great Pacific Garbage Patch exists. As illustrated in figure 6.2, the Great Pacific Garbage Patch is a specific topic embedded within the more general theme of Pollution. But what are the problems associated with the existence of the Great Pacific Garbage Patch?

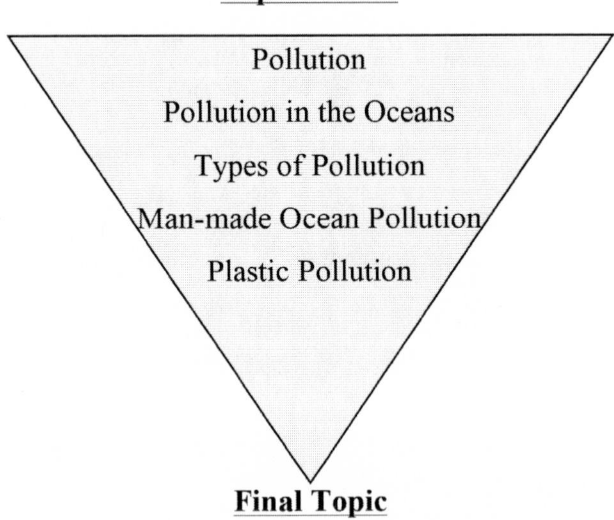

Figure 6.2 Topic Funnel

Problem finding helps students think more precisely about themes and topics and learn how to critique the general theme and go beyond the headlines (e.g., pollution). They learn how to narrow a topic, and then go beyond basic facts to identify specific, nonroutine problems associated with topics. In order to solve a problem one must first find it within a topic. As students move through their final topic they might also recognize layers of topics within their topic by reflecting on the results from their funnel after they find initial problems. Student reflection upon their thinking and revision of ideas is a positive bi-product of the funnel approach to problem finding.

When educators use the funnel approach with students to facilitate their thinking from the general to more specific they are working on a basic form of deductive reasoning; moving from general ideas to more specific ideas. The students cognitively maneuvered their way from the theme of pollution to the specific topic of the Great Pacific Garbage Patch in the above example. The funnel approach is also a concrete application of Vygotsky's *Zone of Proximal Development* in that students who need various degrees of support to engage in more complex thinking have the structure of the funnel and teacher prompts to make learning visible. Conversely, students who need less support can simply arrive at a more specific topic independently and perhaps scaffold beyond to other ideas.

Students and educators can use the funnel approach to find specific problems with their topic and layers of problems within their problems. The process is like a cognitive archeological dig through themes and topics. Thoughtful reflection on funneling can aid students to see the complexity that is naturally embedded in topics and problems and support their thinking to conceptualize the big pictures or connect the dots within topics and problems to see the So What within a topic and problem.

Grade 5 students found the problem listed below for the topic of the Great Pacific Garbage Patch using the funnel approach (see figure 6.3). The problem presented in the figure 6.3 began as a basic thought: *The Great Pacific Garbage Patch is polluting the ocean.* The students funneled their ideas and arrived at their first problem after a series of *how, why*, and *so what*-types of questions and prompts by the teacher, accompanied with some initial exposure to content through three short video clips on the topic.

Although some curricular purists might challenge the quality of the above problem, it represents original and refined thinking on the part of students who worked from a very general topic into a researchable problem. The processes used to facilitate the thinking were (a) evidence-informed and they operationalized the *Zone of Proximal Development*, (b) reflected general principles for unstandardizing curriculum through socially conscious problem solving, and (c) aligned with the Curriculum Paradigm. The cognitive, social, and emotional processes involved on the

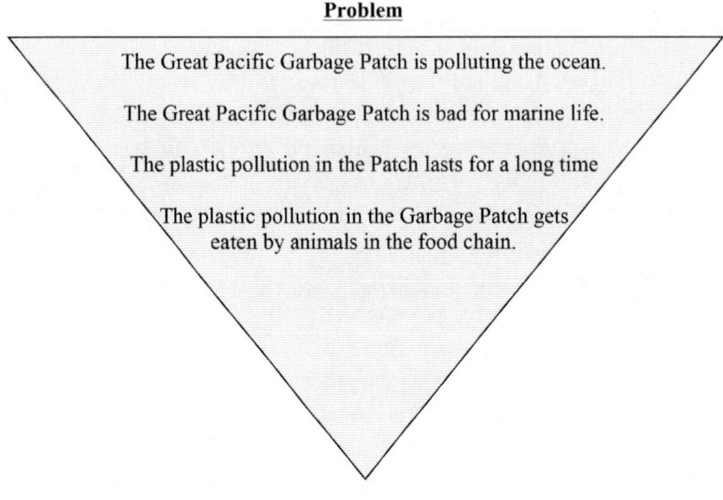

Figure 6.3 Problem Funnel

part of the students when engaged in problem finding are more important than the final product.

The thinking processes and resulting actions on the part of students should be the products. The thinking processes help to prioritize the *What-to-learn content* and operationalize the higher-level skills of *how to learn* by providing students opportunities to experience *So What* and *Now What* thinking and actions. The teacher could have simply assigned a problem from a canned resource but then the various thinking processes and opportunities would have been sacrificed at the altar of efficiency. Students would have been placed in the role of passive receptacle instead of active constructors of meaning as suggested in the Curriculum Paradigm.

The Problem Method

Problem finding is part of a larger approach known as the problem-solving method for organizing and implementing curriculum. The problem-solving method is the scientific method-based process for student learning. It is a multipurpose method that can act as a framework for curriculum design, development and implementation.

The problem-solving method can incorporate the mandated content, *what* students must learn from the curriculum, into a framework for *how to learn*. Problem finding is embedded solidly within the problem-solving method as advocated by Dewey in *Democracy and Education* and other writings (1916; 1933; 1938/1997), and later used to support the curricular processes developed and implemented during the Eight-Year Study (Aikin, 1942) and other landmark works (e.g., Taba, 1962; Tyler, 1949).

The problem method described in Volume II of the Eight-Year Study acts as a framework from which to build and implement curricula from socially conscious topics and a method for learning how to learn as part of experiencing curricula in learning context (Giles, McCutchen, and Zechiel, 1942, p. 15):

1. Define a problem;
2. Formulate a hypothesis;
3. Collect data;
4. Organize data;
5. Draw inferences from data;
6. Recognize the difference between inferences that represent a conclusion or solution to the problem, inferences that demand a restatement of the hypothesis or inferences that demand the formulation of another hypothesis;
7. Translate conclusions into action.

As Dewey (1916; 1933) explained, the problem-solving method as used in the Eight-Year Study requires students to identify (1) a specific problem and then identify facts and knowledge, *the what*, of the problem; (2) the *so what*, or the big picture and significance of the specific problem based on observations, hypotheses generation and mentally wrestling with facts, evidence, and potential outgrowths from layered problems; and the (3) *now what*, hypotheses testing and retesting, formulation and implementation of specific actions to address the problem, and personal connections to the problem.

The addition of two additional overt aspects to the problem-solving method is suggested: (1) Student inquiry into the problem through the formation of student questions about the problem after defining the problem; and (2) Student reflection on the problems associated with the suggested actions or solutions to the problems. Achilles, Reynolds, and Achilles (1997) termed the second aspect as the *problem of the solution*, or considering the consequences of solutions. Student-driven inquiry and reflection help bring purposeful student choice and voice to the problem method.

Student Inquiry

Student generation of questions related to topics and problems is a key feature of the active inquiry process, knowledge acquisition, and knowledge development. Question development allows students to have a degree of input and freedom into what they study and ultimately how they experience the content because the wording of their questions influences the processes and methods used to answer them. The nurturing of student questions is one strategy to facilitate students learning *how to learn* and the inclusion of students' questions allows for a degree of balance between student interest and adult-mandated content. Below are a sample of some questions developed by students about the Great Pacific Garbage Patch and corresponding solutions.

Questions for the Problem:

What are the properties of plastic that make it last a long time and toxic?
How does plastic make its way to the Garbage Patch?
How does plastic affect the food chain?

Questions for Solutions:

What can be done to decrease the amount of plastic in the Garbage Patch?
Who can we collaborate with to solve or address our problem?
What can we do to decrease the amount of plastic we use?
How can we stop plastic from reaching the oceans?
What can we use instead of plastic?

It is incumbent upon the educator to work with the students to create and add more precise questions. Educators can help students refine their thinking about problems by teaching them how to refine their questions. Prompting and clarifying on the part of the educator is an important component to help students refine their thinking and learn *how to learn* within the problem-solving method.

In addition to students developing questions as part of their inquiry, they also develop roles or points of view and specific questions related to their roles and points of view. The students in the Garbage Patch example were prompted by their teacher to think about types of people who would be interested in, study, or otherwise care about the Garbage Patch. The final list created by the students included Oceanographer, Marine Biologist, Animal Rights Activist, Fishermen, Chemist, and Aquatics Vet. The teacher then created a library of developmentally appropriate short videos about each role from the Internet. Students watched the videos to gain a better sense of the roles. Students were then allowed to choose up to two roles.

After students chose their roles they were prompted to create open-ended questions and activities related to the Garbage Patch from the point of view of their role. The questions and activities represented a specialized view of the problem from the point of view of someone with specific interests and knowledge. The strategy used with the students to create their questions was similar to the funnel approach to thinking about the problem. The teacher first prompted the students to think of general questions related to the Garbage Patch. Those questions became the basis for general student inquiry as represented by the initial set of questions presented above. Then the teacher had the students focus on the problem once again, but from a specialized point of view based on their chosen roles.

The strategy of deductive funneling to specificity brought students more directly into the implementation of the curricula through problem finding, inquiry, and reconstructing their understanding via (a) higher-level student introspection, (b) more authentic student voice and choice in defining aims, and (c) eventually the use of multiple measures of evaluation to account for the personalized aspects of the project created by the students. Once again, connecting Dewey's (1916/2009) ideas from *Democracy and Education* about complex thinking as a process to develop unstandardized skills and dispositions necessary for an uncertain future, one can begin to see that having students approach problems from different angles and lenses facilitates the development of overall cognitive nimbleness.

Some examples of student questions and projects from the point of view of the Marine Biologist in Grade 5 included:

How does the oceans' health affect the Earth's environment?
Why is coral important to the life of the ocean?
Plastic Project: Collect data on the amount of plastic my family uses at home, develop ways to use less, try the ways, keep track of use after we try our ideas, plot our data, and make decisions.

A third-grade student involved in the project took on the role of an Animal Rights Activist and asked: where did all the sharks go? She then set out to find the answer. Furthermore, the student proposed creating a video explaining the role of an Animal Rights Activist in addressing the Garbage Patch and the overall health of the shark population impacted by plastic pollution.

So What and *Now What* thinking are embedded in the student questions. The questions in turn provide opportunities for educators and students to design engaging activities that facilitate engagement with unstandardized skills like critical consumption of information, problem solving, big-picture thinking, and taking action. Student questions provide multiple pathways for integrating content from the subject areas of visual art, mathematics, science, social studies, and language arts, to name just a few. The thinking and learning processes are the ultimate products and the subject area content is one vehicle, among many, to help students reconstruct and reorganize their knowledge.

Student Reflection

Students thinking about the problems associated with their proposed solutions add a purposeful reflective aspect to the problem-solving method. Reflection provides openings for students to consider consequences of actions and to weigh various options against criteria. Reflection on the problems of proposed solutions facilitates the creation of a feedback loop because reflection can generate additional student questions and the problems associated with the solutions become new problems for study. Dewey (1916/2009) commented that "every end becomes a means of carrying activity further as soon as it is achieved" (p. 77). The learning never ends. The problems under study can become increasingly layered and extend across grade levels and subject areas. Problems can act as a unifying core from which to organize a school's curriculum.

The students from the Garbage Patch example developed the following reflective questions related to their proposed solutions:

What potential problems for marine life and people are created by our solutions?
Who and what is/are affected positively and negatively by my solutions?
Are the problems created by our solutions acceptable to the marine life and majority of the people involved?
How can we change our solution so that it causes less of a problem but still addresses our original issue?

Reflection is an important component of problem solving because as Achilles, Reynolds, and Achilles (1997) noted, there are always problems associated with solutions. Problem finding and reflection on problems of solutions are integral parts of learning how to learn and engaging with complex issues. Inquiry and reflection are unstandardized skills necessary for life in an uncertain future in a global society. They are important skills and dispositions associated with an overall problem-solving method that is cyclical in nature and incorporates the general principles for unstandardizing (see figure 6.4).

Curricular Flexibility

The Garbage Patch problem as conceptualized by a group of eight- to ten-year-old students, that used the general principles for unstandardizing from the Eight-Year Study and portions of the problem-solving method is one possible problem for the broader theme of pollution. The problem identified by the students is neither too broad nor too specific to inhibit study through the use of integrated subject matter and unstandardized skills and dispositions.

The problem is structured enough to provide a general direction for educators and students to proceed with the development of complex objectives and activities linked to problem-solving method, but pliable or flexible enough to allow for student interest via roles and questions to create multiple pathways of study. Regardless of the pathways implemented, they all end with recommendations for solutions to the original problem/s and reflections on the potential problems with the solutions.

Educators could easily transform the elementary school Garbage Patch problem into a high school unit of study to include advanced chemistry, mathematics, literature, and biology, just to name a few subject areas. Any bureaucratically mandated content standards could also be included, even high school Common Core. However, the Common Core should only constitute the lower-level content for the problem as the vast majority of the

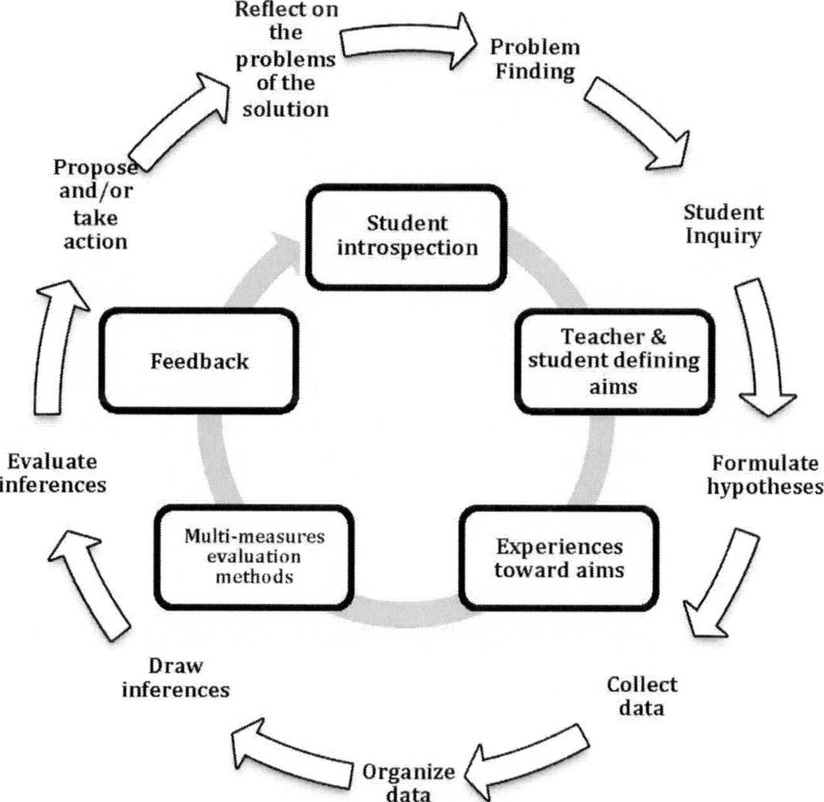

Figure 6.4 General Principles for Unstandardizing Embedded in the Problem-Method Framework.

Common Core high school standards develop only procedural and declarative (lower level) knowledge (Sforza, Tienken, and Kim, 2016).

The take-away point is that "good problems" like the set of unstandardized skills and dispositions presented in chapter 5, transcend time, subject matter, and grade levels. They are persistent problems that are flexible enough to accommodate and develop many levels of complexity and various types of subject-matter content. The open-endedness of complex problems provides unlimited avenues for student inquiry.

The purpose for the inclusion of the above elementary school examples is to demonstrate that even young students can begin to defy standardization and create curriculum that provides more opportunities for free thinking in a short period of time, with some guidance from an educator, in ways that develop complex thinking and align to evidence-informed methods and frameworks. School leaders need not spend hundreds of thousands of dollars on canned standardized programs that deskill and demoralize teachers and reduce them to the equivalent of education automatons while simultaneously extinguishing student choice and voice. The processes educators and students can use to unstandardize curricula are organic, evidence-based, and have the direct effect of increasing the professional capacity of educators while empowering students how to learn.

Complex Objectives

The Garbage Patch problem, as defined by the students, lends itself to the development of complex and divergent learning objectives, like the example cited in the previous chapter from the Asia Society (2015): *Students will take a position based on evidence from sources that considers multiple cultural perspectives and draw actionable conclusions on a globally significant issue/topic.* Similar to the topic and problem, this example objective is flexible enough to be used with elementary school students or high school students.

The objective is not so specific as to detail exactly what students must know, in a specific format and level of emphasis. Instead, the objective allows educators to attach more content-specific objectives to it. The objective can expand in many directions, like the many branches that grow from the trunk of a chestnut tree. The objective does not micromanage the learning, instead it helps to expand curricular and instructional options.

Another example for an open-ended objective for the Garbage Patch, based on an adaptation of the Asia Society (2015) objective, could be: *Students develop collaborative responses, based on empirical evidence from more than one source, that are culturally literate and environmentally responsible, to improve a global problem and assess the merit of their responses based on known and scientifically accepted criteria.* The objective is complex in that it is open ended and does not restrict student thinking to regurgitation and imitation of knowledge. Yet it does not throw out the subject matter baby with the complex thinking bathwater. Students must learn and apply facts and content knowledge to work through the objective.

An example of a complex objective for the Garbage Patch oriented toward mathematics could be the following (adapted from the Asia Society 2015): *Students will develop and implement a viable, manageable, and responsible plan of action supported by the mathematics; and consistent with an argument, conclusion, or decision.* Educators and students can pursue countless mathematics topics in complex ways from this one objective.

Another possible mathematics objective example adapted from the International Society for Technology in Education (ISTE) draft standards (2016) is: *Students will organize and analyze data to make inferences and draw conclusions about problems and potential solutions.* An objective aimed at student reflection that could be paired with a math objective above is adapted from a North American Association for Environmental Education standard (NAAEE, 2010): *Students will explain strengths and weaknesses of proposed solutions and discuss how the proposed solutions could be rejected or their usability improved.*

A potential writing objective related to the Garbage Patch could be something similar to the following objective adapted from the New Zealand Ministry of Education (2009) Grade 7 writing standard (yes, there is only one writing standard for each grade level in New Zealand): *Students will write to develop, record, and communicate experiences, ideas, and/or information related to ways to mitigate plastic pollution.* This objective recognizes that student writing can serve multiple purposes (e.g., develop ideas, record of thinking, communicate ideas and information, and solve problems) and allows for the natural differentiation of student product/output.

Educators can choose to allow for a differentiation of product by simply allowing students to choose various purposes for their writing. Conversely, there are instances when educators might mandate that all students address one specific output embedded in the standards. Educators need to know when to differentiate and when to mandate, but educators are in the best position to make those decisions because they are closest to the students.

The example objectives presented herein work within the general suggestions to unstandardize and within the problem method as presented in figure 6.4. It is possible to integrate almost any K–12 subject content within well-developed topics, problems, and complex objectives. Educators and students need not be limited by one set of bureaucratically mandated standards or standardized curricular processes. Although some behaviorists or proponents of standardization might pan the example objectives as not specific enough or multibarreled (multiple objectives within one objective), the objectives presented, used along with a socially conscious, nonroutine problem like the one identified for the Garbage Patch topic, facilitate curricular opportunities that lead to the development of the unstandardized skills and dispositions necessary for an uncertain future.

Unstandardize to Operationalize the Curriculum Paradigm

The Garbage Patch problem example and corresponding complex objectives presented thus far provide the intellectual and artistic space for educators and students to engage with a full range of unstandardized skills and dispositions when implemented within the problem-method framework. Some skills and dispositions that immediately come to mind for the Garbage Patch example are big-picture thinking, collaboration, cooperation, communicating, conscientiousness, critique, critical consideration of information, curiousness, divergent thinking, environmental stewardship, innovation, leadership, networking building, persistence, problem finding, problem solving, reflection, resilience, social consciousness, stewardship, strategizing, taking action, worldliness, and visioning.

There are opportunities for the development of high-quality learning experiences to engage students in such skills within the example objective adapted from the Asia Society (2015): *Students develop collaborative responses, based on empirical evidence from more than one source, that are culturally literate and environmentally responsible, to improve a global problem and assess the merit of their responses based on known and scientifically accepted criteria.* Readers might find additional unstandardized skills and dispositions to develop via the objective or they might choose different ones. Agreement on the exact skills and dispositions is not important. The importance is in operationalizing unstandardized skills and dispositions within the problem method focused on a socially conscious theme, topic, and/or problem to defy standardization.

The opportunities to organize curriculum as described thus far are only limited by imagination and will. Educators should focus on the "can" possibilities that these ideas provide and not jump immediately to the "I can't" issues. The "I can't" issues will not cease, nor will the need to unstandardize and diversify thinking. Readers are encouraged to use the cognitive energy wasted on "can't" and put it toward "how can we make this happen in some way, on some scale in our learning context?"

The example theme, topic, problem, and corresponding objectives presented in this chapter foster exploration of content in ways that situate students as active constructors of meaning who bring passions, interests, and prior knowledge to the learning situations. The objectives facilitate the organization and implementation (teaching and learning) of the curriculum as a fusion of subject matter and students' personal experiences and interests represented through student voice and choice within the topic and problem development. In other words, the objectives help bring about greater curricular and instructional alignment with the Curriculum Paradigm.

A democratic spirit is allowed to flourish because teachers and students have choice and voice in curricular decisions when using a problem-based approach similar to the one described in this chapter. External forces do not wholly dictate the aims and objectives, nor do they control the instructional processes in the problem method. However, a democratic spirit can be injected into school contexts in which prepackaged standardized programs and dictated aims and processes are the norm by finding opportunities to unstandardize the design, development, and implementation of prepackaged curricula. Admittedly, there are fewer opportunities to unstandardize with prepackaged and scripted curricula, but creative educators can use the ideas from this chapter to make it happen in some way in their contexts.

Educators and students need only repackage the prepackaged programs around socially conscious topics, and problems of interest to them, with complex, divergent objectives so as to loosen the ideological constraints that standardization places on thinking and action. As Dewey (1916/2009) explained, it is imperative for educators to customize curriculum because it must be "constantly growing as it is tested in action . . . and represent a freeing of activities" (p. 76) so as not to become a static list of requirements for educators and students to slog through in mechanistic fashion.

The Problem Method Reconceptualized

A more detailed example of the problem-solving method used for the Garbage Patch example could track along the following path:

1. Define a problem: Topic funneling and problem finding based on student interest and educator knowledge of developmentally appropriate existing problems related to the Garbage Patch.
2. Inquiry: Students and teachers generate an initial set of questions and learning objectives, and then create a refined set after some introductory content exploration and experiences to hone problem solving. The development of questions and objectives can continue throughout the unit of study so the unit evolves organically, yet it is tied to the core topic, problems, and objectives.
3. Formulate a hypothesis: Students generate and reformulate hypothesis about causes and consequences based on initial understandings of the problems and after some introductory content so as to refine hypotheses generation.

4. Collect data: Content from standards, curricula, subject matter, and data from scientific sources.
5. Organize data: Categorize information according to the student and teacher-generated questions. Present data in ways that communicate knowledge of the information under study (e.g., journals, videos, essays, presentations, models, public service announcements, etc.)
6. Draw inferences from data: "So What" meaning making, big-picture thinking, and connecting the dots to see associations between the problems, the content, the individual, and the world.
7. Recognize the difference between inferences that represent a conclusion or solution to the problem, inferences that demand a restatement of the hypothesis, or inferences that demand the formulation of another hypothesis: Identify inferences that lead to hypotheses reformation, problem expansion, additional problem finding, and conclusions. Provide for differentiated degrees of analysis of the big pictures and the analyses can lead to the development of actions.
8. Translate conclusions into action: "Now What" can I do, can we do, about this?
9. Problems of the actions: Reflective thinking about consequences of solutions. What problems are possible because of our solutions and how can we improve solutions to lesson problems?

The above reconceptualization of the problem method is not meant to be a recipe as much as it is a guide. Processes will vary as will the emphasis given to each part of the method when organizing curriculum and when using the problem method as teaching and learning processes. It is within the natural variation of processes that a diversity of learning springs forth and the cognitive nimbleness of students and artistry of educators are allowed to flourish. If all educators do the same things, in the same way, with the same level of emphasis, then they are no longer unstandardized because students experience sameness of process without diversity of method or activities. There is no progress through standardization.

It is as Dewey (1916/2009) stated, "For only diversity makes change and progress" (p. 68). Curricular diversity is a cultural hallmark of American public school, as noted by Rugg (1927): "Local option in school practice; each state and each chartered city was left free to make its own course of study. . . . By 1890 diversity was becoming a characteristic of the American public school system" (p. 36). Rugg described the natural processes that led to the idea of incubators of innovation referenced earlier in the book in which each class, within each school, within each school district in each state is an incubator of innovation and unstandardized skills and disposition, guided by the Curriculum Paradigm.

The problem method can be the core or the skeleton of the curricular operation that provides the consistency that some educators and policy makers crave, like a security blanket to sleep at night. Yet the problem method provides flexibility to diversify topics, problems, skills, dispositions and experiences. Although skeletons consist of the same core material (e.g., bone), the external features that create the final outward appearance of the human being are infinitely different and diverse. The problem method provides a structure from which to develop a universal core for curriculum, but it is flexible enough to allow for creative expression and experience of that core.

Tips for Themes, Topics, Problems

Educators can foster the development of unstandardized skills and dispositions more effectively through the strategic development of themes, topics, and/or problems with students. Not all themes, topics, or problems are created equal in that they do not all lend themselves to complex thinking or the infusion of integrated subject matter. Some are not flexible enough to transcend subject matter or to facilitate a diverse set of skills or dispositions.

Some evidence-based characteristics of themes, topics, and problems (e.g., Dewey, 1902; Caswell and Cambpell, 1935; Dewey, 1902; Giles, McCutchen, and Zechiel, 1942; Stratemeyer, 1957; Tyler, 1949) aligned to the Curriculum Paradigm include: (a) facilitate student study of socially conscious problems associated with democracy or the global community; (b) represent topics of interest and/or are familiar in some way to a wide range of students; (c) are ongoing or recurring in nature so that they remain current and important; (d) transcend subject matter and allow for the integration of diverse content and methods; (e) facilitate cooperation, collaboration, and communication among educators and students; (f) are potentially controversial in that multiple points of view exist; (g) are divergent in nature and allow for multiple solutions and processes to arrive at solutions; (h) can traverse several grade levels or grade bands to create a scaffolded core of study; (i) do not require specialized resources or extra funding that would make their study onerous; and (j) can be accomplished within existing confines of the school such as schedules, staffing, budget, and facilities.

Attending to the evidence-based characteristics for themes, topics, and problems keeps educators moving toward forms of curricula and instruction that facilitate unstandardized functions. If one wants to achieve different results, one must do things differently. Education policy has been ignoring the Curriculum Paradigm and the complementary functions of public school for some time. If educators, community members, and students want to change the current standardized trajectory of education policy, then they must do things differently; they must unstandardize.

Building a Customized Core from the Theme Up

Existing curriculum standards or mandated standardized curriculum objectives and content can be integrated into the problem-solving method and the study of almost any socially conscious problems. Socially conscious problems are also fertile ground for the development of locally nurtured, yet globally informed, curricular objectives, standards, and assessments. The reader should not interpret the problem method as the equivalent to curricular Groundhog Day in which educators and students reinvent the curricular wheel or must develop original topics and corresponding problems each year.

Educators in each grade level or grade spans can accumulate reusable problems, from common topics, over time through discussion and brainstorming with students and make those problems part of the curriculum during a five-year curriculum renewal cycle. High-interest themes, funneled to carefully selected topics, combined with well-defined problems can form the organizational basis for an entire school curriculum for grades K–12. The broad themes, like pollution, leadership, sustainability, can remain the same for each grade but the specific topics, problems, subject matter content, and complexity and foci of the objectives for those themes can change to reflect developmentally appropriate levels of cognition and social and emotional learning.

The linear interpretation of the approach presented thus far, exemplified in figure 6.5, might be an appropriate jumping off point to begin to unstandardize curricula and instruction. The linear interpretation could work well for educators and other interested parties who have difficulty imagining how to organize a less standardized curriculum from multiple perspectives. Likewise the linear interpretation can serve the needs of those who seek the security of a perceived orderly approach to facilitate curriculum development.

The collaboratively identified general themes, like pollution, can act as a unifying structure, a core if you will from which to organize curriculum. The specific topics, such as the Garbage Patch, with its corresponding problems, objectives and student-driven questions and reflections can act to customize the core at each grade level or age range to the interests and passions of the students compelled to experience it. Thus, a level of standardization can exist through the themes that run through multiple grade levels (e.g., all grades study pollution), but customization of implementation is guaranteed throughout the processes of unit design, instruction, and classroom assessment.

Curiously absent from the approach to unstandardizing depicted in figure 6.5 is any mention of subject-matter content. It is purposefully not included in the model because content is not the product, it is merely a vehicle, among other vehicles to foster complex thinking and learning experiences. Any subject-matter content can be integrated into the process on the back end after themes, topics, problems, and a starter set of divergent objectives have been determined. Starting from content only increases the chances that the students will be made to fit a standardized plan instead of having authentic choice and voice in the learning.

Even the linear approach to unstandardizing allows for students to have meaningful choice and voice in the curriculum each year by identifying additional problems, objectives and questions they want to explore and study for existing problems that have already been adopted into the local curriculum. As time passes, school personnel can slowly replace standardized and discipline-centered curricula with problem-based curricula options that provide more consistent opportunities to develop unstandardized skills and dispositions. The degree and speed at which that happens is a local decision based on local needs, resources, interests, skills, and passions.

Next-level Unstandardizing

The linear approach to the design, development, and implementation of unstandardized curricula is limiting and should only be used as a starting point if necessary. Curriculum design and development can begin with themes, objectives, problems, or topics. There is not a strict order from which one must start. The curriculum designer is only constricted by his/her education imagination (Eisner, 2001). As noted by the likes of Dewey (1916/2009) ,Tyler (1949), and

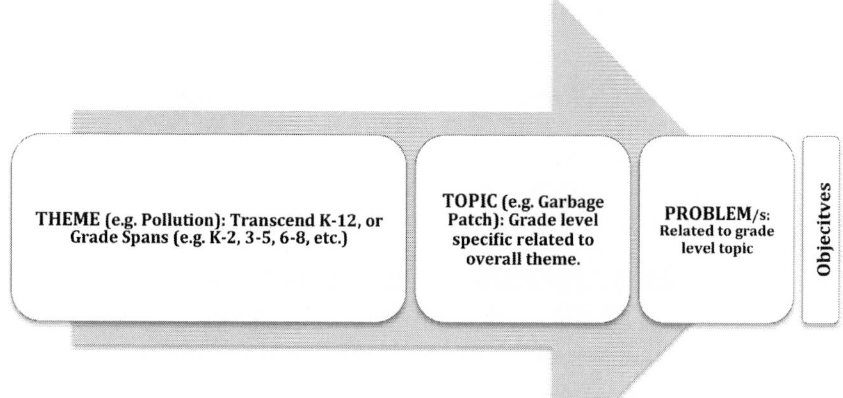

Figure 6.5 Linear Approach to Unstandardizing

Taba (1962), curriculum design and development should be an organic process approached from different angles and perspectives.

Problems can develop from topics just as topics can flow from a problem. An important aspect of the problem method, and the aspect that aligns well with the Curriculum Paradigm is that students must participate in the finding and solving of problems (Giles, McCutchen, and Zechiel, 1942). Educators and students think and imagine in different ways. The curriculum development and design processes should respect the varied thinking processes and voices brought by each party.

Naturally Differentiated

The problem method to organize and implement curriculum is naturally differentiated for students by cognitive, social, and emotional developmental readiness, learning process, product, student interest, and content because of the open-ended, divergent way that content is conceptualized and organized. The focus should not be solely on all students arriving at the same answer. Instead, the focus of the problem method is the processes students use to arrive at solutions to problems and the appropriateness of those solutions given the problems and contexts.

Likewise, the problem method is naturally differentiated for educators because it allows for science and artistry to coalesce into original learning designs (Eisner, 2001). Yes, different classes within the same grade levels could potentially arrive at different final products because the problems are open ended, multifaceted, and support the development of multiple solutions. That fact is congruent with allowing teacher and student voice and choice in the development of the curriculum. The degree to which that happens should be a local decision.

School personnel might choose to decide on a core of subject-matter content for each unit, represented by state-mandated curriculum standards, locally mandated content, and/or other sources of curriculum. Subject domain content exists. For example, linear equations in algebra exist. The problem method does not do away with recognized content, it simply allows for democratic input into how that content is experienced in terms of emphasis, format, and level of difficulty.

School personnel can use predetermined content as the anchor for each problem study and use the teacher and student questions and problem statements as the differentiating factors to customize the experiences. The blending of predetermined content with differentiated design and implementation is one way to defy standardization. The artistry with which content and facts are integrated is dependent on the design entrepreneurship of those creating the curriculum.

Next Steps

Educators have options in the ways they unstandardize curricula. Multiple pathways exist to organize content to engage students in diverse curricula experiences that align to the Curriculum Paradigm and address the complementary functions of public school. Educators need not be overwhelmed with which pathway to choose or worry about being perfect in their choices of pathways or implementation; they just need to focus on being better.

Although educators might seek perfection in curriculum design, development, and implementation, "you can't always get what you want, but if you try sometimes you just might find you get what you need" (Jagger and Richards, 1969). Do not let the drive to develop perfect curricula be the enemy of designing better curricula. As Gawande (2007) stated, "Better is possible. It does not take genius. It takes diligence. It takes moral clarity. It takes ingenuity. And above all, it takes a willingness to try" (p. 246).

REFERENCES

Achilles, C.M., Reynolds, J., & Achilles, S. (1997). *Problem analysis.* Philadelphia, PA: Routledge.

Aikin, W.M. (1942). *The story of the eight-year study.* New York: Harper.

Asia Society. (2015). *Graduation performance system.* Author. Retrieved from http://asiasociety.org/competence/leadership-global-competence.

Caldwell, O.W. (1927). The Lincoln experimental school. In H. Rugg (Ed.), *Part I curriculum making past and present, The twenty-sixth yearbook of the National Society for the study of education* (pp. 271–289). Bloomington, IN: Public School Publishing.

Caswell, H.L. & Campbell, D.S. (1935). *Curriculum development.* New York: American Book Company.

Dewey, J. (1902). *The child and the curriculum.* Chicago: University of Chicago Press.

Dewey, J. (1916). *Democracy and education.* New York: McMillan.

Dewey, J. (1933). *How we think* (2nd ed.). Lexington, MA: D.C. Heath.

Dewey, J. (1938/1997). *Experience and education.* New York: Touchstone.

Dewey, J. (1916/2009). *Democracy and education: An introduction to the philosophy of education.* Cedar Lake, MI: Readaclassic.

Eisner, E.W. (2001). *The educational imagination: On the design and evaluation of school programs* (3rd ed.). Upper Saddle River: Pearson.

Gawande, A. (2008). *Better: A surgeon's notes on performance.* New York: Macmillan.

Giles, H.H., McCutchen, S.P., & Zechiel, A.N. (1942). *Adventures in American education volume II: Exploring the curriculum.* New York: Harper and Brothers.

International Society for Technology in Education. (2016) *Draft standards for students.* Author. Retrieved from https://docs.google.com/document/d/1r9KATQ_X6JPTuS0NxQS3LlAsC96UZr3wsUftg_RuYBM/edit.

Jagger, M. & Richards, K. (1969). You can't always get what you want. *Let it bleed.* London Records.

Jersild, A.T., Thorndike, R.L., & Goldman, B. (1941). A further comparison of pupils in "activity" and "non-activity" schools. *Journal of Experimental Education, 9*, 307–309.

New Zealand Ministry of Education. (2009). *Reading and writing standards.* Author. Retrieved from http://nzcurriculum.tki.org.nz/National-Standards/Reading-and-writing-standards/The-standards/End-of-year-7#2.

North American Association for Environmental Education [NAAEE]. (2010). *Excellence in environmental education: Guidelines for learning K-12.* Author. Retrieved from http://resources.spaces3.com/89c197bf-e630-42b0-ad9a-91f0bc55c72d.pdf.

Rugg, H. (Ed.). (1927). Three decades of mental discipline. Curriculum-making via national committees. In *Part I curriculum making past and present, the twenty-sixth yearbook of the national society for the study of education.* Bloomington, IN: Public School Publishing, 33–65.

Sforza, D., Tienken, C.H., & Kim, E. (2016). A comparison of higher-order thinking in the grades 9–12 Common Core State Standards and the 2009 New Jersey content standards for English language arts and mathematics. *AASA Journal of Scholarship and Practice, 12*(4), 4–32.

Stratemeyer, F. (1957). *Developing a curriculum for modern living* (2nd ed.). New York: Teachers College Press.

Taba, H. (1962). *Curriculum development: Theory into practice.* New York: Harcourt, Brace, & World, Inc.

Tanner, D. & Tanner, L. (2007). *Curriculum development: Theory into practice.* Upper Saddle River, NJ: Pearson.

Thorndike, E.L. (1924). Mental discipline in high school studies. *Journal of Educational Psychology, 15*, 1–22, 98.

Tramaglini, T.W. & Tienken, C.H. (2016). Customized curriculum and high achievement in high poverty schools. In C. Tienken & C. Mullen (Eds.), *Education policy perils: Tackling the tough issues* (pp. 75–101). Philadelphia, PA: Taylor Francis.

Tyler, R.W. (1949). *Basic principles of curriculum and instruction.* Chicago: University of Chicago Press.

Wang, M.C., Haertel, G.D., & Walberg, H.J. (1993). Toward a knowledge base for school learning. *Review of Educational Research, 63*(3), 249–294.

Wrightstone, J.W. (1935). *Appraisal of newer practices in selected public schools.* New York: Teachers College Press.

Wrightstone, J.W., Rechetnick, J., McCall, W.A., & Loftus, J.J. (1939). Measuring social performance factors in activity control schools of New York City. *Teachers College Record, 40*(5), 423–432.

Vygotsky, L. (1978). *Mind in society: The development of higher psychological processes.* Cambridge, MA: Harvard University Press.

Chapter 7

Structure for the Long Term

Readers might have recognized multiple pathways to organize content included in the problem-method examples presented in chapter 6. For example, the unit approach and student-needs approach were integrated in the examples. There were also characteristics of a formal structure to organize curricula on a larger scale: the problem-focused core. Educators can embed the unit and student-needs approaches into the larger organizing structure of a problem-focused core as a mechanism for long-term curriculum renewal and organization. The core can be used to organize integrated curriculum for an entire class, grade level, school, or district.

The approaches to curriculum development illustrated in the examples in chapter 6 share some characteristics that educators can apply to organize and diversify curriculum on a large scale: (1) The approaches can be used to develop new curricula or to restructure any existing curriculum; (2) there is a purposeful focus on socially conscious problems and democratic action; and (3) the approaches move curriculum design, development, and implementation toward alignment with the Curriculum Paradigm in ways that are familiar to educators. This chapter describes a formal structure and various approaches to organize unstandardized curricula on a larger scale and it presents examples and ideas for implementation.

APPROACHES TO ORGANIZING CURRICULUM ON A LARGE SCALE

The Great Pacific Garbage Patch example presented in chapter 6 could be categorized as a unit approach to organizing content because it represented

a single unit of study that educators developed to organize and implement subject-matter content, skills, and dispositions. Conversely, educators could categorize the Patch example as a student-needs approach to curriculum design because the topic is of high interest to students and it potentially affects their lives. Likewise, readers might connect the consistent and overt references to socially conscious problems made in chapter 6 to a problem-focused core approach. The Garbage Patch example has aspects of all three characterizations: (a) unit approach, (b) student-needs approach, and (c) problem-focused core. It represents a blended model of curriculum design, development, and implementation. The blending of approaches to organize content in the Garbage Patch example was intentional because the processes used to design, develop, and implement curricula do not have to be standardized nor perfect, they just have to be better than what existed previously.

Facing Reality

Some curriculum purists might argue that there is one best way to design, develop, and implement curriculum. They might call for a problem-focused core in which subject-area boundaries are totally eclipsed and content is fully integrated. Perhaps that is the perfect way to organize curricula; around socially conscious problems without specific subject-area constraints such as standardized tests and subject grades necessary for calculating grade point averages and class ranks. But sometimes the best solution is not always the first possible solution and progress should not halt because perfection cannot be attained on the first try.

Should educators move the design, development, and implementation of curricula in the direction of a fully integrated problem-focused core? The evidence from over 150 years of research and professionally informed practice suggest the answer to that question is yes in order to fully operationalize the functions of public school in a democracy. However, bureaucratic constraints such as testing and grading policies imposed in some states and school districts might make achieving *perfect* curricula organization difficult at first.

The development of a purely problem-focused core might never occur in some schools. But should bureaucratic constraints be allowed to deny the pursuit of unstandardized curricular progress aligned to the Curriculum Paradigm and the complementary functions of public school? No. Educators need only to move forward toward better curriculum design, development and implementation, in the direction of perfection.

Curriculum design and development might not achieve perfection according to the purists, but most curriculum purists do not work in K–12 settings. As long as public school educators are moving toward greater integration of subject matter, skills, and dispositions around socially

conscious problems then progress is achieved. There is growth as long as there is progress.

The speed and scope with which educators can move toward unstandardized curriculum integration will depend on what Lewin (1951) termed the driving forces facilitating curriculum renewal and the restraining forces inhibiting it in the contexts in which educators find themselves. Some schools, in some school districts, in some states have more restraining forces than others. The speed and depth at which they will be able to defy standardization will vary. There is not a standardized protocol or time limit on the process of diversifying curriculum. The key for educators is to just keep moving forward toward less standardized teaching and learning processes and experiences for educators and students by blending approaches.

Units of Study

A unit of study approach is as it sounds. Educators develop independent units of study based on selected skills, content, themes, topics, problems, and objectives. The units can be self-contained, one-time-only events in a grade level or classroom, or they can be connected to a series of units around the same theme that spans a grade level or multiple grade levels. For example, the Garbage Patch could be a single unit and be the only unit students experience on the topic of pollution as part of a middle school science class. Conversely, the Garbage Patch could be a unit in one grade level that is part of a ten-year cycle of single units focused on pollution that span grades 1 through 10. Each unit in each grade level would address a different type of pollution and integrate different content, problems, topics, skills, and dispositions but retain the same theme in the case of a multiyear cycle of units.

One weakness of the unit approach is that the units do not have to be based on open-ended, socially conscious themes, topics, or problems. They can be myopically focused on isolated skills if educators do not make concerted efforts to include socially conscious problems and unstandardized skills and dispositions. Surely some readers have seen, been made to use, or been a part of writing a nonsocially conscious, close-ended unit such as one on punctuation marks for instance. A subject-centered, socially inert unit would be the antithesis of what is proposed in this book, but it could be used as an example of what not to do when leading curriculum design and development efforts.

It is important to use the problem method, aligned to the Curriculum Paradigm, and focus on integration of content as part of the process, not the final product, when using the unit approach. The content is not the end result. Content is part of an overall process that integrates content, skills, and disposition into a problem-focused framework. Units can become standardized when service to static content is the primary purpose.

Student Needs

A student-needs approach to curriculum design, development, and implementation places the student at the forefront of the learning process. Educators who use a student-needs approach view curriculum and instruction through a lens of the major concerns of students in terms of themes, topics of interest, problems, and the instructional methods used to meet students' unique learning needs. The curriculum is constructed around pressing student needs. Students are part of the curricular decision-making and they are engaged in active, socially connected learning, as part of a student-needs approach.

An intrepid group of educators from Des Moines pioneered the development of the student-needs approach on a large scale in 1938 as part of their curricular and instructional experimentation during the Eight-Year Study. They sought to incorporate issues relevant to students' lives in the present and not only focus on issues related to their lives as adults. Topics included Making a Living, Protecting Life and Health, and Cooperating in Social and Civic Action (Giles, McCutchen, and Zechiel, 1942, p. 74). Although the units developed by the Des Moines educators were topics specifically related to student needs, they were not superficial in nature nor did they represent low-level learning. They transcended time in that they could be studied for multiple years, across multiple decades.

The topics used in Des Moines allowed educators to integrate subject-matter content around socially conscious problems. The topics facilitated the development of learning experiences that provided students opportunities to learn and use unstandardized skills and dispositions. Giles, McCutchen, and Zechiel (1942) summarized the approach used by the Des Moines teachers:

> Adolescents need training and practice in reaching intelligent decisions and in effective social participation. How can such training better be given than by group consideration of matters of as vital concern to them as what they will study and how they will study it? (p. 73)

Some readers might describe the student-needs approach as student-centered or learner-centered. They might use the words *voice* and *choice* to describe the role of the student in some of the decision-making about curricula and the way they interact with content. Those are valid descriptions but it is important to note that a key aspect of the student-needs approach is student voice and choice into what is learned, not only how some of the ways students experience the learning.

The approach developed by the teachers in Des Moines in 1938 goes beyond a differentiated choice board activity in which students get to choose from a set of preselected, teacher-generated activities. In the Des Moines approach, students were able to be part of the process that decided unit themes, topics, problems, and the instructional methods. The Des Moines approach to student-centered curriculum is in contrast to the current conception of student-centered or student needs. The current thinking about student needs is a bit narrow and often ends with students only getting to choose the order in which they complete predetermined standardized activities or a choice of activities from a preset menu. That is not to say that low-level student choice is not important. It is, but authentic choice and voice put students as partners with the design, development, and implementation processes.

This is not to say that students should have full command of the content and methods of the curricula. That would represent a misguided approach based on the flawed philosophy of Romantic Naturalism, in which students drive what is learned, how and when things are learn, based on felt needs. For example, students learn math when they feel the urge to learn math. Dewey (1902) warned against such a view when he stated, "As long as we confine our gaze to what the child here and now puts forth, we are confused and misled" (p. 18).

Dewey knew the difference between having students be part of the process as opposed to students determining the complete education process and outcomes. Understanding the student-needs approach is useful in helping educators keep a focus on the student so as not to forget to include the students in decision-making. But the use of the student-needs approach does not mean students do whatever they want to do when they want to do it.

The essence of the student-needs approach was used in the Garbage Patch example without falling into the trap of only playing to students' felt needs as described by Dewey. Specifically, the inclusion of student ideas for topics and themes, along with the participation of students in determining some of the problems and questions for inquiry, brought the students actively into the curriculum development and implementation. An aspect of providing students authentic choice and voice is teaching them how to be actively involved in academic work.

There are multiple opportunities within the Garbage Patch example specifically, and the problem method more generally, to include students in meaningful ways so they engage in the "training and practice in reaching intelligent decisions and in effective social participation" (Giles, McCutchen, and Zechiel, 1942, p. 72) brought about by unstandardized curricula design, development, and implementation.

Problem-Focused Core

The problem-focused core can act as an overarching structure from which to organize curricula (Tanner and Tanner, 2007). The problem-focused core is a structure that can be used to organize a micro-curriculum, such as one course, but its full strength is operationalized when used to organize a macro-curriculum, like a high school subject area or an entire program of studies. The problem-focused core is a structure, which in its purist form, is designed to blur subject-matter boundaries (Tanner and Tanner, 2007, p. 262).

Subject-area content is fully integrated around socially conscious problems that transcend grade levels and form a unified focus of themes that flow through curricula. Subject-matter content such as mathematics is one vehicle, among others, to engage in socially conscious problem solving. Mathematics is not an end in itself. The use of unstandardized skills and dispositions along with subject-area content to solve socially conscious problems is the end game.

A weakness with the problem-focused core is that the curricular purists' view on its operationalization is difficult to achieve in public schools given the unending bureaucratic micromanagement that continues to mandate that educators teach and assess content in isolated silos and contrived bits of information. But educators and students can reimagine the problem-focused core as a tool to reorganize courses, content areas, or a complete curriculum. By focusing on socially conscious themes, topics, and problems, educators and students can transform the way curricula is designed, developed, and implemented but still include the mandated subject matter.

Reimagining curriculum through the use of a problem-focused core is more unstandardized and aligned to the Curriculum Paradigm. The problem-focused core is situated on a foundation of evidence and informed professional judgment. Educators and students can feel secure in knowing they are collaborating with curriculum giants like Dewey when they engage in designing, developing, and implementing a problem-focused core.

The Garbage Patch is one example of a way to build a problem-focused core. Although it was originally designed as a single unit of study, the Garbage Patch represents one piece of a larger curricular theme that can carry through a school; the theme of pollution. Educators can use the theme to organize an entire science course for a grade level or as one theme among several from which to organize an entire science program or an entire curricular program in which subject matter is integrated frequently.

Likewise, pollution could be one theme, among others, around which educators and students in an entire school decide to organize the curricula for all the grade levels in the school. For instance, the La Paz Community School, an international, bilingual PK–12 school located in the Guanacaste region of Costa Rica, organizes the entire school curricula around eight themes and most of the subject-matter content is taught within those themes:

1. Peace Ambassadors
2. Sustainability

3. Origins
4. Land and Sea
5. Wellness
6. Energy
7. Creative Expression
8. Gratitude

Content areas exist at the La Paz Community School. There are mathematics classes, science classes, etc., but the organization of the content for those classes at each grade level revolves partially around the eight socially conscious themes and identified problems within the themes. Subject-area lines blur more often in the La Paz curricula because the educators there communicate about the themes and they work with students to develop and revise projects in each subject area that reflect the themes and integrate other subject areas. The educators weave unstandardized skills and dispositions into each of the themes and projects at each grade level.

The La Paz Community School must still meet the standardized high school graduation requirements set forth by the Costa Rican Ministry of Education in order to award high school diplomas. Furthermore, the school uses a two-way English / Spanish immersion approach and participates in the International Baccalaureate Program™ at the high school level and that program has its own set of standardized curricular and assessment mandates similar to some levied by state education bureaucrats in the United States. But the ways in which La Paz educators meet those requirements are more unstandardized and more aligned to the Curriculum Paradigm and complementary functions of public school than not. The educators at La Paz are focused on progress and building better curriculum programs and practices. They are not paralyzed by the unrealistic standardized pursuit of perfect, and thus the curricular program moves forward and produces enriching learning experiences for students.

PUTTING IT ALL TOGETHER

Educators and students can organize curricula with fidelity to the Curriculum Paradigm and the complementary functions of public education around a problem-focused core by linking a series of socially conscious themes, topics, and problems connected to student needs, around units of work that permeate multiple grade levels. Educators can begin the process almost immediately by using their existing units and adding a problem focus if one does not already exist.

The power of the problem-focused core is harnessed when it acts as an overarching organizing structure for curricula through multiple grade levels or an entire school, like it does at La Paz. However, even a single educator can harness the power of the problem-focused core to unstandardize and transform his or her class. Progress comes in all degrees and speeds. Don't let the pursuit of perfect curricula paralyze movement toward better curricula.

Brainstorming Beginnings

Educators and students can begin the process of developing a cohesive, unstandardized problem-focused core for a class, grade level, or a school by brainstorming groups of problems, topics, and/or themes with students and putting them into theme-based categories, or theme buckets, such as Environment, Personal Health, Conflict, and Economics. Educators and students can compare the categories within their class, grade, or among grade levels to identify commonalities that carry through to create a common stream of themes, topics, and problems from which to build the multigrade problem-focused core.

Because the problem-focused core proposed in this chapter is based on linked units, it is an easily recognizable structure to most educators who have had at least one class on curriculum design. Even educators who go through crash course programs without the benefit of formal collegiate coursework on curriculum can quickly understand what comprises a unit of work and thus build larger curricular structures from there. For example, if an educator extends the Garbage Patch example beyond one unit in one class, to an elementary school, the path to a problem-focused core becomes clearer. For instance, another group of educators that used the Garbage Patch in their school also found that students in multiple grade levels consistently raised themes, topics, and problems related to pollution during brainstorm sessions.

One result of a brainstorming session held within grades K through 5 uncovered hundreds of comments, some of which coalesced around pollution: (a) trash in our town; (b) when I walk to school I have to walk through dirty streets; (c) dirty water, like in Flint, Michigan, and Newark, New Jersey, makes people sick; (d) pollution in our town is bad for me; (e) pollution on the land and sea is dangerous for animals; and (f) how does pollution affect our food? Any of the student comments listed could act as a unifying theme from which to design a problem-focused core through the development of units.

One might conclude from the initial student responses that there was simplistic thinking from the brainstorming session, but that conclusion is deceptive. The six brainstormed examples presented above represent potential themes, topics, and problems aligned to a potential large-scale problem focus. The brainstorming session is only a first step educators use to tap into student needs and interests. It is the opening to authentic student choice and voice in the later development of socially conscious units. Educators can then link the units together to form a problem-focused core. The process of refining student thinking through prompting is a thinking product in itself educators can use throughout the process.

Open-Ended Funneling

Upon further reflection it can be seen that the students in the school from the example were clearly interested in themes, topics, and problems connected to pollution, among other things. After identifying the possible multigrade-level theme of pollution, the educators followed the problem method introduced in chapter 6 and used the funneling approach with students to arrive at a list of more specific topics for grades K through 5, focused on the theme of pollution:

- Kindergarten: A Clean Classroom
- Grade 1: Keeping Our Community Clean
- Grade 2: Pollution in Our World
- Grade 3: Clean Earth, Safe Food
- Grade 4: The Great Pacific Garbage Patch
- Grade 5: The Triple Threat: Cars, Fossil Fuels, and Solvents

The educators made the conscious decision to follow a structured funnel approach from theme to topic. They could have chosen to move from theme to problem, and then to topic, or they could have started with finding problems. As noted in chapter 6, educators can use a linear approach that starts with theme and then moves to topic, problems, and objectives. Educators can also use a more organic approach in which they use problems, topics, and themes concurrently that arise from student brainstorming. The exercise the educators in the example used of funneling to topics from student brainstorming was connected to student needs and socially conscious thinking in that the brainstorming session was wide open in terms of allowing students to state topics, themes, problems, or even questions.

The educators did not stunt student creativity during the process by mandating that students only provide answers related to themes. They used a democratic brainstorming approach and allowed open-ended, divergent, creative thinking to flourish organically. As a result they indirectly provided opportunities to engage in the development of unstandardized skills and dispositions such as active listening, brainstorming, communicating, creativity, critique, divergent thinking, imagination, and social consciousness.

After the brainstorming phase, the educators used a strategy to organize and sharpen the student thinking and make it visible by working with students to categorize their ideas into buckets of themes, topics, and problems. Students understand more about their thinking when they see it visually.

Educators can use visual brainstorm webs or other methods that students can see to help them think more about their thinking and thus help them develop metacognition strategies.

Focusing on a Core

A problem-focused core begins to take shape at the point when educators and students identify problems, based on a common theme, that connect the curriculum of a class, such as ninth-grade biology, an entire grade level, or multiple grade levels. The topics and problems focused on the pollution theme connect through every grade in the elementary school and integrate multiple subject areas. After coalescing around a theme, educators and students can use the funneling approach to arrive at specific topics and/or problems for each grade level, some of which might be similar among some grade levels. Some of the potential topics and problems might also emerge during the initial brainstorming sessions. Educators should keep a record of the brainstorming sessions and categorize the responses for use developing future themes, topics, and problems.

After educators and students arrive at topics and problems, they can begin to develop the frameworks for specific integrated units of work that will fill out the core and represent the actual curriculum documents. The units of work will contain the themes, topics, problems, complex objectives, content, and learning activities that will be implemented with the students. The exact format and organization should be left to the discretion of the educators, but generally problem-focused units contain (a) a description of the overarching theme and topic so educators and students can gain a general perspective of how the unit should be approached, (b) descriptions of the problem/s, (c) complex learning objectives, (d) in depth descriptions of activities, (e) examples of nonroutine teaching resources like differentiated activities, (d) complex writing and activity prompts, and (e) live-links to web-based resources.

A description of the overarching theme is important so as to provide context. For example, the educators who developed the Garbage Patch unit used the perspective of an environmental steward. They implemented the unit from the perspective that the Patch is an environmental problem that needs to be addressed on multiple fronts. The unit explored ideas such as reducing the use of plastics, questioning the way plastics are currently used for all types of packaging, recycling procedures, political lobbying for changes in plastics laws, and disincentives for people to use plastics.

The students would have experienced the unit differently if it was implemented from the point of view of the plastics industry. The focus would most likely have been to continue use plastics unabated but address the problem more indirectly by more litter control and the development of plastics that decompose faster. One perspective is not better than another for the purposes of learning.

A more comprehensive way to deal with the issue of perspective is to offer both sides of the issue but help students to evaluate each side based on scientific facts and standards of ethics. That approach affords students the chance to critique information and arguments based on science and evidence and can teach them about the tensions that exist between ideological thinking and scientific evidence and ethical behavior. For instance, scientific evidence suggests that faster decomposing plastics would not solve the problem because plastic does not biodegrade into natural products, it photo-degrades into smaller particles made of chemicals that are unhealthy for marine life and humans.

Stabilizing and Filling a Core

The educators involved in the Great Pacific Garbage Patch topic eventually used it as an overall organizer for the entire Grade-4 curricula. They integrated content throughout the Grade-4 program by using problem-based learning activities tied to the topic. Problem-based learning derives from activities based on ill-structured problems, what Dewey (1938) termed "indeterminate situations" (p. 108). Ill-structured problems are not easily solved. They are messy, controversial, constantly evolving, and require students to examine the problem from many angles in order to better understand it. That is why they are "indeterminate" in nature. The activities used for problem-based learning should capitalize on the opportunities inherent in the approach to allow for divergent and complex thinking based on the problem method introduced in chapter 6.

The activities used to fill a core should lead students to more complete and complex understandings of the problem. Students can construct and reconstruct their knowledge and skills as they progress through the study of the problem. The recursive nature of problem-based learning allows for hypothesis testing and reformulation, reflection, reconstituting of knowledge, and the development and testing of solutions that are increasingly complex. Dewey (1938) noted that "as the problem progressively assumes a more definite shape by means of repeated acts of observation, possible solutions suggest themselves" (p. 108). Problem-based learning is a process for learning, and it is the process that is an important product of the problem-focused core.

The Garbage Patch problem ultimately found by the Grade-4 students presented in chapter 6 was: *The man-made plastic pollution found in the Great Pacific Garbage Patch will last for hundreds of years and threaten the marine life in the North Pacific and contaminate the food we eat.* The problem acts as the pivot point for studies at all grade levels. The identified problem attaches to the larger theme that runs through the entire K–5 program: pollution. The problem also links to related topics in each grade level (e.g., the Garbage Patch in Grade 4) and specific problems for each grade level.

Content area divisions begin to blur at the point of problem finding and they can evaporate in earnest during the development of complex objectives related to the problem. Consider a revised example of a complex objective presented in chapter 6 that was adapted from the Asia Society (2015): *Students develop collaborative responses, based on empirical evidence from more than one source, that are culturally literate and environmentally responsible, to address the Great Pacific Garbage Patch locally, regionally, and globally, and assess the merit of their responses based on known and scientifically accepted criteria.* This example objective can be used in Grade 4, but it can also be used as an anchor objective to tie the curricula of all the grade levels together by simply changing out *Garbage Patch* for the other grade-level topics. Then the problem-focused core is linked at the themes and objectives thereby creating stronger curricular linkages across grade levels.

The problem-focused core envelops multiple grade levels as the themes, topics, problems, and objectives are purposefully developed to connect. Consider the following example of the beginnings of an unstandardized problem-focused core:

K–5 Theme: Pollution
K–5 Topics:

- Kindergarten: A Clean Classroom
- Grade 1: Keeping Our Community Clean
- Grade 2: Pollution in Our World
- Grade 3: Clean Earth, Safe Food
- Grade 4: The Great Pacific Garbage Patch
- Grade 5: The Triple Threat of Cars, Energy, and Solvents

K–5 Problems:

- Kindergarten: *Dirty classrooms can cause us health and safety problems.*
- Grade 1: *The man-made pollution found in our community can last for many years and cause health problems for animals and people.*
- Grade 2: *The man-made pollution found around the world will last for hundreds of years and cause health problems for animals and people.*
- Grade 3: *The man-made pollution found around the world will last for hundreds of years and threatens our health and the quality of the food we eat.*

- Grade 4: *The man-made plastic pollution found in the Great Pacific Garbage Patch will last for hundreds of years and threaten the marine life in the North Pacific and contaminate the food we eat.*
- Grade 5: *The man-made pollution from cars, energy production, and solvent cleaners will last for hundreds of years and threaten air, water, and climate of Earth and change life for its inhabitants.*

K–5 Problem-focused Core Anchor Objective

- *Students develop collaborative responses, based on empirical evidence from more than one source, that are culturally literate and environmentally responsible, to address (Put the specific topic here) and assess the merit of their responses based on known and scientifically accepted criteria.*

Complex problems and objectives can anchor an entire unit or an entire year of study. There are multiple objectives and activities that can arise from them. Educators and students can decide how encompassing to make their problems and objectives for the problem-focused core. But educators should give thought to the amount of time necessary to engage in the problem method and meaningful activities to truly operationalize the definition of curriculum presented earlier in this book as the "reconstruction of knowledge and experience that enables the learner to grow in exercising intelligent control of subsequent knowledge and experience" (Tanner and Tanner, 2007, p. 99)

Nurturing the Core

The framework for the problem-focused core is established as each grade level develops their topics, problems, and an anchor objective. The core grows as educators and students add units of study that include related objectives, activities, projects, and resources. The units are supported by the general principles of unstandardizing and the problem method. The number of units added depends on whether the topic spans one unit, one semester, one year, or multiple years. That decision rests with educators and students.

Educators will not finish the example problems and objectives presented in this chapter during a class-period activity. The problems and objectives will snowball into other problems and objectives if developed and implemented correctly. They will spark students to continue their studies long after the themes and formal school activities are completed. Educators need not worry about *covering it all*. Yes, there will be state-mandated content that must be integrated, and there will be many additional topics that educators might want to also introduce. But perhaps less is more in this case.

Educators should go deeper with the experiences and make each theme like a cliffhanger, to be continued, so that students can use their knowledge, skills, dispositions, and other resources to continue to quench their thirst for more learning.

The complex problem and objective presented in the examples represents the problem-based heart of the problem-focused core. Educators and students can build activities that address pieces of the larger problem and objective, and when completed, the activities add up to a portfolio of activities all aimed at addressing the problem while simultaneously integrating subject-area content and unstandardized skills and dispositions.

Multiple free or inexpensive resources exist for ideas for problem-based learning activities that educators can use to help nurture a problem-focused core. One such resource is a free site I curate that has over seventy websites with problem-based examples. It can be found at: http://www.scoop.it/t/problem-based-learning-by-christopher-tienken. The site is a good starting point for ideas and existing problem-based activities.

Educators and students can create their own resource sites for their curricula and activities and attach those sites to the formal school district curricula, pending formal school board approval. Including practical resources for problems and activities in the school district curricula increases the chances that people will use the curricula because it becomes more practical to use. All of the units and activities should be part of the formally approved curricula so that the curricula become a clearinghouse for unstandardized learning.

On the Shoulders of Giants

The educators who developed the examples presented in this chapter and in chapter 6 are operating in a highly structured, evidence-informed, innovative manner. They designed curricula and learning experiences aligned to the Curriculum Paradigm. The curricula and activities simultaneously addressed the complementary functions of a public school and provide opportunities for students to experience and use unstandardized skills and dispositions without being rigid or mechanistic.

The educators are standing on the shoulders of giants like John Dewey, Harold Rugg, Ralph Tyler, Hilda Taba, Wilford Aikin, Francis Parker, and other intrepid progressive-experimentalist educators, exiting the cave of standardization. Educators who engage in unstandardizing are forging new pathways through their use of the progressive-experimentalist principles as "stars as trails to lead them out" (DeLonge, 2007). The educators are no longer operating unconsciously; they are heeding Coniglione's (2015, p. 21) words and they not only know *what* to watch and *how* to see in terms of curriculum development and implementation, but they know how to operationalize the Curriculum Paradigm and unstandardize for the future.

Defy Standardization and Change the Future

The fetish with authoritarian standardized policies and practices is undermining the democratic fabric of the country because it is undermining the overall quality and functions of the public school system. Educators and students can make lasting and impactful changes to the intellectual oppression caused by mass standardization. Curricula expectations and output do not have to be standardized. Fear mongers and standardization followers masquerading as education leaders and reformers need not halt progress toward better education opportunities for all students. Educators at the local level have it within their power to defy standardization and change the trajectory of education for millions of students.

If educators work to unstandardize their programs to whatever degree possible, within the context they work, they will allow students to experience progress. Little steps add up to leaps. As noted by Smith and Tyler (1942, p. 11), the "fundamental purpose of schooling is to affect changes in students" and it is the design and development of curricula embedded with unstandardized skills and dispositions, organized around a problem-focused core, and aligned to the Curriculum Paradigm, that produces those changes. Curricula, and schooling in general, should be and can be unstandardized.

Educators can find inspiration in the words of Robert F. Kennedy's *Day of Affirmation Speech* (1966) as they can work as lone citizens or in small groups to take the small steps that will collectively change the course of education for millions of students:

> Few will have the greatness to bend history itself, but each of us can work to change a small portion of events. . . . It is from numberless diverse acts of courage and beliefs that human history is shaped. Each time a man stands up for an ideal, or acts to improve the lot of others, or strikes out against injustice, he sends forth a tiny ripple of hope, and crossing each other from a million different centers of energy and daring those ripples build a current which can sweep down the mightiest walls of oppression and resistance.

Educators can work with students and community members to make ripples throughout the curricula. Over time the ripples result in a sea change within the educational experience for students that change lives.

THOUGHTS

A universal set of performance-guarantee curriculum standards for all students: public education's saving grace or just another empty promise based on junk science and ideology? The answer is clear. Educators and students can do better than mindlessly following cognitively and socially static curricula, built on nineteenth-century ideas that will create knowledge imitators and automatons. Why must educators, students, and community members settle for an outdated education aimed at targets that no longer exist?

Educators can do better than subject students to myths, fears, and lies about a lack of global competitiveness. Educators can foster the pursuit of skills and dispositions that transcend centuries and careers. They do not need to be afraid of other countries' education systems or believe in myths about being cognitively dominated by a foreign power. Educators do not need to standardize and homogenize children. Educators can expand, enrich, and diversify curriculum locally while thinking globally. Defy standardization: today's students will thank you in 2060.

Next Steps

What happens next on the path to defying standardization and creating curriculum for an uncertain future depends on what you, the reader, decide to do with the information presented herein. Lead, don't follow. Be patient, but don't wait. Create the next ripple.

REFERENCES

Coniglione, F. (2015) Introduzione. Complessità del reale, semplicità del pensiero. In I. Licata (Ed.), *I gatti di Wiener. Riflessioni sistemiche sulla complessità*. Bonanno Editore: Acireale-Roma 2015, p. 21.

DeLonge, T. (2007). Heaven. *I-Empire* [CD]. Los Angles: Geffen Records.

Dewey, J. (1938). *Logic: The theory of inquiry*. New York: Holt, Rinehart and Winston.

Dewey, J. (1902). *The child and the curriculum*. Chicago: University of Chicago Press.

Giles, H.H., McCutchen, S.P., & Zechiel, A.N. (1942). *Adventures in American education volume II: Exploring the curriculum*. New York: Harper and Brothers.

Kennedy, R.F. (1966). Day of affirmation. Speech at the University of Cape Town, South Africa. Retrieved from https://www.youtube.com/watch?v=yp81OYCjXtU.

Lewin, K. (1951). *Field theory in social sciences*. New York: Harper & Row.

Smith & Tyler, R. (1942). *Adventures in American education volume III: Appraising and recording student progress*. New York: Harper and Brothers.

Tanner, D. & Tanner, L. (2007). *Curriculum development: Theory into practice*. Upper Saddle River, NJ: Pearson.

Index

About the Author

Christopher H. Tienken, EdD, is an associate professor of leadership, management, and policy and education consultant. He has public school administration experience as a PK–12 assistant superintendent, middle school principal, director of curriculum and instruction, and elementary school assistant principal. He began his career in education as an elementary school teacher. Tienken is the former editor of the *American Association of School Administrators Journal of Scholarship and Practice* and the current editor of the *Kappa Delta Pi Record.* Tienken's research interests include school reform issues such as standardization, the influence of curriculum quality on student outcomes, and the construct validity of high-stakes standardized tests as decision-making tools. He was invited to be a member of the Professors of Curriculum organization in 2015 and was named the 2014 College of Education and Human Services Researcher of the Year. Tienken received the Truman Kelley Award for Outstanding Scholarship from Kappa Delta Pi in 2013. The Institute of Education Sciences recognized his research about the effects of professional development on student achievement and the National Staff Development Council (Learning Forward) awarded him the Best Research Award in 2008. Tienken has authored over eighty publications including book chapters and articles. His book, with co-author Don Orlich is titled, *The School Reform Landscape: Fraud, Myth, and Lies*. His book, with Carol Mullen, is *Education Policy Perils: Tackling the Tough Issues.* He presents papers regularly at state, national, international, and private venues. Tienken has ongoing research collaborations with colleagues at the Universita` degli Studi Roma Tre, Rome, Italy, the University of Catania, Sicily, and he was named as a visiting professor at both universities.